PAUL

ESSENT

Joscelyn Godwin
was born in England in 1945 and has written, edited and translated
several books on the Western esoteric tradition, metaphysics,
alchemy and music. He currently teaches at Colgate University in
New York State and visited Paul Brunton a number of times in the
1970s.

Paul Cash and **Timothy Smith**
worked closely with Paul Brunton in his later years, seeing him daily
in his retirement in Switzerland and helping him to organize some
10,000 pages of notes. After his death they headed the team of
editors responsible for the sixteen-volume *The Notebooks of Paul
Brunton* (1984-89).

PAUL BRUNTON

ESSENTIAL READINGS

Selected and edited by
JOSCELYN GODWIN
with PAUL CASH and TIMOTHY SMITH

First published 1990

British Library Cataloguing in
Publication Data

Brunton, Paul, *1898-1981*
Paul Brunton.
1. Religious life. Mysticism
I. Title   II. Godwin, Joscelyn
III. Cash, Paul
IV. Smith, Timothy   V. Series
291.422

ISBN 1-85274-080-9

*Crucible is an imprint of The Aquarian
Press, part of the Thorsons Publishing
Group, Wellingborough,
Northamptonshire, NN8 2RQ, England*

Printed in Great Britain by Mackays
of Chatham, Kent
Typesetting by MJL Limited,
Hitchin, Herts

1 3 5 7 9 10 8 6 4 2

ESSENTIAL READINGS

The *Essential Readings* series is designed as an introduction to the life and works of major figures in the history of ideas, particularly in the realm of metaphysics and the esoteric tradition. This anthology of Paul Brunton's writings is a most welcome addition to those volumes in the series devoted to modern figures. As a twentieth-century mystic and savant Paul Brunton successfully communicated to many readers a broad range of spiritual experience, drawing upon his profound study and practice of meditation and his encounters with holy men of the East.

Paul Brunton travelled widely in India and Egypt during the 1930s and met with several leading Indian sages and gurus, otherwise inaccessible to Western visitors in that period. From these meetings he garnered much original spiritual wisdom, which he determined to impart in his books published between 1934 and 1939. His fluent and readable style eschews complex jargon and exotic terminology. His accounts of spiritual training and progress emphasize experience, mood, and atmosphere; he bids his reader accompany him on an inner journey of adventure into the soul and provides clear practical guidance.

The kernel of his mature teachings reflects traditional Neo-Platonism with their insistence on the discovery of the soul, the divine atom in the heart, which represents the Godhead and its eternal wisdom (i.e. the Overself) in each mortal human being. In his later books *The Quest of the Overself* and *The Wisdom of the Overself* Brunton documents the timeless truths of mysticism and self-knowledge in the context of the divine aspect of humanity and its purpose.

What makes this anthology exceptional is that the editors had first-hand knowledge of the man. Joscelyn Godwin, who was first introduced to the ideas of Brunton by Anthony Damiani, visited him in Switzerland on five occasions between 1970 and 1980, while Paul Cash and Timothy Smith spent months with him and were responsible for the meticulous edition of his Notebooks between 1984 and 1989. Brunton touched each of their lives and this personal inspiration is manifest in their contributions to the anthology.

Paul Brunton wrote of the Sphinx that 'it surveys no earthly landscape. Its unflinching gaze is always directed inwards and the secret of its inscrutable smile is self-knowledge.' In this sense, Brunton was himself a little sphinx-like. He never set himself up as a guru or cult leader, nor indulged in mystifications regarding his own person or his writings. He acted more as an exemplar, an ambassador for the spiritual truths and higher realities. Thus he interested and attracted his readers and, it is hoped through this anthology, will continue to do so.

NICHOLAS GOODRICK-CLARKE
November 1989

CONTENTS

INTRODUCTION

The soul of Paul Brunton 'exchanged a tranquil existence for a troubled one' (as he puts it) somewhere in London in the year 1898. We cannot tell anything about his family background, his education, even his name at birth, for 'P.B.' (as he preferred to be called) did not share them with his readers or visitors. His twenty-eight books offer scant aid and less encouragement to a biographer. But this is of small moment in comparison with the panorama they unfold of the inward and spiritual quest to which his entire life was dedicated. Respecting his own sense of proportion, therefore, this introduction is based exclusively on what P.B. chose to tell his readers about himself, often incorporating his actual words.

P.B. tells us that his first intimations of the quest came in boyhood through reading: he mentions the inspiration he found in St Paul's letters, Bulwer-Lytton's occult novel *Zanoni*, and especially *The Awakening of the Soul* (or *Hai Ebn Yokdan, the Self-Taught Philosopher*) by Ibun Tufail. It was the latter, a Sufi work, that gave P.B. the general idea of meditation, a subject on which he would become the foremost modern authority. Unguided, uninstructed, he began to practise, groping his way in what at first was absolute darkness. After six months of daily meditation, and eighteen months of burning aspiration for the Spiritual Self, he underwent a series of mystical ecstasies.

The glamour and freshness of these youthful illuminations subsided after a few weeks, but left P.B. with a continual awareness which he carried within him for a further three years. P.B. now met an advanced mystic, an American living in London, who invited him to undergo certain tests that, if passed, would lead him on to the next degree of illumination. The result was a failure, and P.B. entered thereupon into the state called by the medieval mystics the Dark Night of the Soul. For three years he had neither time nor capacity to meditate, or even to sustain aspiration.

An unexpected event shocked P.B. out of his spiritual depression. He again took up the practice of meditation, and after some weeks recovered, in a memorable session, the degree of consciousness that he had earlier enjoyed. But now it was with increased knowledge and understanding. He began to see clearly the patterns and significances behind his own life and those of others. He realized that throughout his dark years, the spiritual Presence had never abandoned him, but had silently awaited the time when his own efforts would reunite him with it. He drew from this the great lesson of the necessity of hope, and, more than that, felt charged with the task of communicating it to others who might feel discouraged by their lack of success on the quest.

Years of development and growth followed this second illumination. For many months during 1918, P.B. heard what he calls the 'Interior Word', realizing that the source of strength and wisdom was not to be sought anywhere but in one's innermost Self.

After the First World War, P.B. lived for a time in Bloomsbury. He shared a flat with Michael Juste, founder of the Atlantis Bookshop, in the very house that Virginia and Leonard Woolf would later make their home and that of the Hogarth Press. Having always been a natural, even a compulsive writer, P.B. now entered the world of journalism, and became a successful editor and writer of publicity material.

At the end of the 1920s P.B. embarked on intensive research on the Orient, carried on with the help of the Secretary of State for India's library. Thus prepared, he set out on his first journey to the East. During 1930-1 he travelled in India, mixing with all classes and meeting yogis, fakirs, and holy men and women of every degree. The two for whom he felt the deepest kinship were the Shankaracharya of Kamakoti and Sri Ramana Maharshi, the Sage of Arunachala (not to be confused with Maharishee Mahesh Yogi). The Shankaracharya, spiritual head of South India and the inheritor of the Vedantic lineage founded by the first Shankara, was born in 1895 and is still living as I write this in 1989; in fact, he has been seen in public *darshan* reading P.B.'s Notebooks. As the head of a public institution, he declined to take P.B. as a pupil, but suggested that he go to Arunachala, a holy mountain in the extreme south of India, and meet a sage who lived there. This was Ramana Maharshi, then virtually unknown, now celebrated as a rare modern representative of the purest Advaitin (non-dualist) school of philosophy and self-realization.

P.B.'s search for the spiritual treasures of India found its climax in the meeting with Ramana Maharshi. As he presents it in his book, *A Search in Secret India*, he then began an inward search under the sage's direction. Through meditation on the question 'Who Am I?' he discovered that he was not the body; not the emotions; not the intellect. Eventually, as can be read in our extract, he was left with the thoughtless state of pure Being, that allowed a higher, unsuspected Self to take over. This alone was perfect freedom. In point of fact, as he tells us much later in the Notebooks, this was no new experience to P.B., but a renewed contact with the state he had known years before.

While in India, P.B. contracted blackwater fever which enervated him for two years. On his recovery he refused the many offers that came his way of lucrative editorial and publicity work and set out to turn his Indian experiences into a book. He settled in a quiet South Buckinghamshire village, staying in two rooms over the village inn until a cottage of his own was built. Nearby was a historic Friends' meeting-house, where P.B. would go each Sunday, finding among the Quakers and their worship qualities wanting in other Christian denominations.

A Search in Secret India presents its author as somewhat sceptical and naïve, but it must be understood that this was a pose, consciously adopted to appeal to sceptical and naïve readers of the 1930s. This was still the era of Empire, when colonialism and the Christian missionary movement had schooled the British to an ingrained contempt for the brown man and his religions. But here was a traveller who not only witnessed phenomena that baffled materialistic science, not only dared to praise Islam as a socially laudable and rational religion, but who ended up sitting awestruck at the feet of a loin-clothed yogi. For the Foreword, P.B. called on Sir Francis Younghusband, co-leader of the British expeditionary force that had invaded Tibet in 1904 and now, in his retirement, devoted to the reconciliation of world religions. The book was enthusiastically received and sold a quarter of a million copies in several languages.

On two distinct occasions after his return from India P.B. received in meditation a solemn charge or mission. One summer evening on the bank of the Thames, he was plunged into deep trance and entered the presence of the Four Great Beings who watch over the spiritual welfare of the planet. A special task was given to him, both frightening and exalting. Again, in 1934, when about to leave on his second journey to the East, he received an urging from the sage he had known there to share with others his knowledge of the path that leads to the spiritual Self. Putting his travel arrangements aside, he responded by writing *The Secret Path* in only four weeks. Alice A. Bailey contributed a Foreword to it, and the book was published in 1935.

The Secret Path is a short manual of meditation, one of the first to appear in the modern West and the very first to explain the Self-enquiry method as taught by Ramana Maharshi. Here P.B. establishes one of his firmest principles: no matter how mystical or abstruse his material, always to explain it in plain English. One searches his works in vain for the learned footnotes, the untranslated Sanskrit, Chinese, and Tibetan terms that adorn the scholarly literature and frighten away the non-academic reader. What P.B. learned from the Orient and from ancient tradition, he presents as a living wisdom, as precious to the factory worker as to the professor. This style of presentation naturally removed him from consideration by the academic world, while certain reviewers were moved to extremes of abuse. He reflects on this reception in the prefaces to some of his books.

P.B. began his second voyage with a period in Egypt, where he collected the materials and underwent the strange experiences chronicled in *A Search in Secret Egypt*. This is the most sensational of his works, touching on occult history and the Atlantean origins of Egyptian civilization and monuments as well as on present-day magicians. We open this selection with the account of the night P.B. spent inside the Great Pyramid. Equipped with stronger nerves than most of his readers, he seems to have re-enacted the process of initiation which the Pyramid was originally intended to serve. This demonstrated to the neophyte, beyond all doubt, the immortality of his being and his ultimate freedom from the material world.

P.B.'s two 'Searches' pay homage to the twin sources of modern esotericism. On the one hand there is Egypt, home of the Pyramid builders and of the Hermetic tradition: the Egypt which regarded the ancient Greeks as children, and to which their philosophers went for initiation. Alchemy, Gnosticism, Freemasonry, and the Western magical tradition all trace their roots to Egypt. On the other hand there is India, discovered by the West late in its history, source of the Vedas and of the *Bhagavad Gita*, home of Krishna and of Gautama the Buddha. The esoteric doctrines of India had come to the wider attention of the West with the Theosophical Society of the late nineteenth century. It was for P.B. to demystify them and to provide a practical adaptation of yoga (the way of becoming 'yoked' to God—the root word is the same) for ordinary people.

Continuing his journey, P.B. sailed from Egypt to India and again reached the ashram of Ramana Maharshi before the end of 1935. One day, on climbing to the top of the sacred mountain of Arunachala, P.B felt prompted to address his fellows in the West, whom he could see spiralling ever downwards into a purposeless materialism. Forthwith he wrote down the substance of a short book, which like his later Notebooks is not a continuous argument or narrative but a series of loosely-connected paragraphs. *A Message from Arun-*

achala is a serious call to the Western world to attend to its soul. In later years, P.B. would regret that the tone of the book had been so negative, but it well reflects the clouds that were gathering over Europe at the time of its writing.

In the summer of 1936, P.B. made a retreat in a small bungalow high in the Himalayas, as the guest of a Nepalese prince. Out of this came perhaps his most beautiful book, *A Hermit in the Himalayas*, which is full of his love of unspoilt nature and his kinship with the stars. Here he speaks most intimately to the reader, dropping the mask he created for the two 'Searches' and showing himself living the simple and solitary life that he preferred, moving gradually, as he puts it, 'into the courts of the Lord'.

The next summer it was the Maharajah of Mysore who offered P.B. hospitality and the conditions favourable for the writing of *The Quest of the Overself*. The Maharajah was a most enlightened ruler and a devotee of non-dualist Vedanta. His patronage of P.B., together with the friendship of the Maharajah's Reader in Philosophy, T. Subrahmanya Iyer, and of T.M.P. Mahadevan, Professor of Philosophy at Madras University, gave the lie to P.B.'s Indian and Western critics who maintained that through writing popular books he had watered down or misrepresented Eastern doctrines. Often the motive behind such criticisms stemmed from P.B.'s refusal to endorse someone's favourite guru, or to lend his energies to political movements. Those who taught and lived the highest philosophy, like Ramana Maharshi, the Shankaracharya, and Sri Atmananda, instinctively accepted him as one of their own. *The Quest of the Overself* is a successor to *The Secret Path*, being a more detailed manual of meditation. It contains many exercises designed to appeal to people of different temperaments and needs. We extract from it a passage on 'The Overself in Action', in which P.B. explains—as he would do, time and again—that meditation and the inward quest are not for making monks and hermits, but for the support and centering of those living an active, normal life in the Western world.

It was also in 1937, and at the Maharajah of Mysore's behest, that P.B. made a special study of the echoes of Eastern wisdom in Western philosophy. This appeared as *Indian Philosophy and Modern Culture,* a short study that, alone among P.B.'s books, has not been reprinted for many years.

The last fruit of this Indian period was *The Inner Reality* (titled in its American edition *Discover Yourself*), written in 1938. The specific purpose of this book was to address Christians, and to introduce them to the deeper meanings of their religion and to the benefits of meditational practice. There are fascinating and original commentaries on the Beatitudes, the Lord's Prayer, etc., in the light of the quest. It is from here that we draw P.B.'s words on Jesus as portrayed in St John's Gospel.

In 1938, P.B. left the East for the USA, where he spent some months. From the West Coast he sailed back to Asia, visiting China, Siam, and Cambodia before settling again in India for the duration of the Second World War. It was in 1939 that he came to the ruins of Angkor in Cambodia, once the seat of a high and spiritual civilization that had blended harmoniously Hinduism and Buddhism. P.B. had gone there, like Madame Blavatsky before him, in order to receive a certain contact through meditation; he alludes to this on page 115 of this book. But another contact was made there, in the flesh, that would be of great significance to him. This was with an exiled Mongolian lama, who was able to answer some important metaphysical questions. Thanks to the key furnished by this Mongolian, P.B. was able to embark on his philosophical masterwork.

The ambitious project of a two-volume work that would explain in plain language the highest philosophy and its concomitant practices was eventually divided, to P.B.'s regret, into two separate books, *The Hidden Teaching Beyond Yoga* and *The Wisdom of the Overself.* Many who had enjoyed the P.B. of the earlier writings were disappointed in them, for these books were, frankly, difficult reading. Those who persisted learned that beyond the rewards of religious devotion, beyond the ecstasies of mysticism, lies the realm of true Philosophy, a term to which P.B. restores its noble meaning of the 'love of wisdom'. He explains why it is not sufficient to have psychic or even spiritual experiences: one must understand what one is experiencing, or else run the risk of the self-deception, the imbalance, or the dogmatism for which mysticism is no cure—indeed, to which psychics and mystics have often been given. The 'hidden teaching beyond yoga' is the wisdom that knows why one practises yoga (or meditation, for P.B. almost never concerns himself with Hatha or physical yoga). It is cosmological wisdom that knows how the world comes into being; how we perceive it; and why the world is the way that it is.

The first volume, *The Hidden Teaching Beyond Yoga*, leads the reader step by minute step to the admission that the material world as it is commonly conceived simply cannot be said to exist. The second volume, *The Wisdom of the Overself*, supplies the solution to this impasse in the adoption of a purely 'mentalistic' philosophy. It explains how our whole world is projected by our own minds, and how the greater world outside us is projected as a thought by the World-Mind. It is an achievement of a rare order to have expounded this subtle and revolutionary doctrine without jargon and without a plethora of difficult terms. P.B. reduces the uncontrolled richness of Eastern philosophy to a few monumental concepts, of which the most important ones are as follows: the Ego, the illusory and separate being which each of us thinks we are; the Overself, which is our divine reality; the World-Mind, creator of all universes; and Mind in itself, the silent and unmanifest ground of all being.

It is impossible to convey adequately the majesty of *The Wisdom of the Overself*; the poignancy of its chapters on suffering, death, and the current world war; the supreme value of the practical exercises in mental yoga, which are found nowhere else in Western literature. Above all, there is the transformative effect of its philosophy, like water to one dying of thirst in the desert of modern pseudo-philosophy. An extract is given here from the heart of the book, where P.B. explains 'The Birth of the Universe' as a thought in the World-Mind.

P.B. finished *The Wisdom of the Overself* in December 1942. He had written ten books in less than ten years, and now he fell so silent that notices were published of his death. He left India at the end of the war, and his subsequent travels took him again around the world, though we cannot trace them more exactly. A man like P.B. is never idle, even though he may pass a year or more being seen to do nothing but eat a little, and sleep less. The quest continues in realms which we cannot imagine, and the burden of helping humanity, once accepted, may take strange and inward forms.

In 1952 he broke his silence, publishing *The Spiritual Crisis of Man*. This was the first book since *A Search in Secret India* which he had been able to write at leisure, and the Notebooks contain hundreds of additional paragraphs that must come from this period. The 'spiritual crisis' of the title is reducible to the question: Is the human race going to learn its lesson from two world wars, or is it going to plunge through ignorance into a third disaster even more terrible? The book is a reflection on the spiritual consequences of the Second World War and on the only direction in which future hope lies: that of humanity's return to moral and spiritual principles. More than that, it is a work of inspiration to the individual who has set foot on the path of return but is obliged to live among those who ignore or refuse it.

The Spiritual Crisis of Man was the last book that P.B. published in his lifetime. The following year, 1953, he himself went through a crisis. He had fallen ill of a tropical malady, contracted in the Far East, that threatened to end fatally. Falling into a coma, he encountered the astral figure of a well-known and well-loved Master, who gave him the choice between putting his body aside then and there, or of recovering and continuing his earthly life for the benefit of his fellow humans. Out of pity for those who looked to him for help, P.B. reluctantly decided to return and complete his mission.

Always fated to be a wanderer, P.B. continued to travel. He stayed for two years in New Zealand; he spent time in Australia and the United States. He consistently refused invitations to set himself up as a public figure, or even to be made the focus of a private ashram as Ramana Maharshi had been. Eventually he settled in Switzerland, living mainly on the shores of Lake Lugano and Lake Geneva. He treasured his solitude, and protected it from the importunities of the well-meaning and the half-crazy alike by maintaining only a postal address. Occasionally he would consent to give interviews, but only on condition that the seeker was not hoping to find in him a guru. Shopping and cooking for himself, facing the rigours of the Alpine winter—these became increasingly burdensome as he neared his eighties. In his last years, friends ensured that he always had an assistant on call, to look after domestic chores and write letters for him.

Some of what P.B. had been doing during his silent years emerged when it was realized that he had written some seven thousand pages of notes, together with three thousand pages of related research materials, deliberately withholding them from publication until after his death. Apparently P.B. had scarcely passed a day without writing something, in obedience to his chosen profession and his lifelong habit. But far from being a connected discourse or treatise, these notes seemed to have been made at random, on every conceivable subject. They ranged from single sentences to substantial paragraphs; there were also a few essays of a page or more in length. In stark contrast to their physical nature—for they were often written on tiny scraps of paper or in cheap lined notebooks—the notes showed a deepening of the philosophy that had been expounded in the published books, reflecting the very considerable changes through which P.B. had gone since his silence.

When a few friends of P.B. learned of the existence of this material they were concerned that it should not be lost, besides being most eager to read what he referred to vaguely as his 'Summing Up'. A group of Americans who had been introduced to his work by Anthony Damiani, founder of Wisdom's Goldenrod Philosophic Center, was permitted to start typing and sorting these notes with a view to their eventual publication. By the time P.B. died on 27 July 1981, he had established twenty-eight categories under which to classify this material. The manuscripts were removed to Valois, on Seneca Lake, New York, where intensive work on them went forward. A collection of essays, apparently dating from the 1940s and 1950s, was published in 1984 as *Essays on the*

Quest, and the same year the first volume of the Notebooks, *Perspectives*, appeared under the imprint of Larson Publications. The singleminded devotion of a few dozen people and their financial supporters enabled the series of Notebooks to be published with unprecedented speed, the sixteenth and last volume appearing in 1989.

The task of selecting from these sixteen volumes what seems 'essential' to the reader, who may or may not go on to explore P.B.'s other writings, has been undertaken by Paul Cash and Timothy Smith, whose editorial responsibility for the Notebooks has given them an unrivalled knowledge of the material. Somewhere P.B. writes: 'These disconnected sentences of mine are like beads waiting to be properly matched and strung together on a string'; the stringing has been the work of the Editor. The guiding principle in our selection has been to answer the question of why this man's life and work are important. To this end, our choices from the Notebooks have tried to show how a sage approaches the human situation and how he describes, in retrospect, the spiritual quest that has brought him to this state. What makes a sage different from other men and women? What makes him the same as every one of us?

To pose these questions, in this context, is to suggest that Paul Brunton was himself a sage: an enlightened or liberated man, or a *jivan mukti* if one prefers the precision of the Hindu term. Note, however, that the claim is ours, not his. It is not a false modesty that makes him steer carefully away from asserting his own enlightenment, while writing with unprecedented clarity about the state of consciousness of the man who has reached the goal of the human quest. It is inherent in the very thing that makes a man a sage: that he has permanently vanquished his ego, and has no longer any sense of personal identity beyond what he may assume for convenience or courtesy. He lives in union with the Overself, which has never achieved enlightenment for the simple reason that its eternal essence is enlightenment. From that standpoint, he is describing a process and a state of which he has no sense of possession. The knowledge that this is also the destiny of every one of us seems to be as essential as anything that can be got by reading.

It only remains to thank those who have allowed the free use of Paul Brunton's copyrighted works: Kenneth Thurston Hurst, Esq., Samuel Weiser, Inc., and Century Hutchinson Publishing Group, Ltd. Royalties from this book are being given to the Paul Brunton Philosophic Foundation, P.O. Box 89, Hector, New York 14841.

JOSCELYN GODWIN

PART ONE

READINGS FROM BOOKS PUBLISHED IN PAUL BRUNTON'S LIFETIME

1

A NIGHT IN THE GREAT PYRAMID

From *A Search in Secret Egypt* (London: Rider & Co., 1936), p. 65-78. (In USA: 2nd edn. rev., York Beach, ME: Samuel Weiser, 1984. Copyright 1984 Kenneth T. Hurst.) Used by permission of the publisher and Mr Hurst.

Paul Brunton has obtained permission to spend the night inside the Great Pyramid of Cheops in Giza. Having explored the various passages and chambers by torchlight, he settles down in the King's Chamber.

The minutes slowly dragged themselves along, the while I slowly 'sensed' that the King's Chamber possessed a very strong atmosphere of its own, an atmosphere which I can only call 'psychic'. For I had deliberately made myself receptive in mind, passive in feeling and negative in attitude, so that I might become a perfect register of whatever super-physical event might transpire. I wanted no personal prejudice or preconception to interfere with the reception of anything that might come to me from some source inaccessible to the five physical senses of man. I gradually diminished the flow of thoughts until the mind entered a half-blank state.

And the stillness which descended on my brain rendered me acutely cognizant of the stillness which had descended on my life. The world, with its noise and bustle, was now as utterly remote as though it did not exist. No sound, no whisper, came to me out of the darkness. Silence is the real sovereign of the kingdom of the Pyramid, a silence that began in prehistoric antiquity and which no babble of visiting tourists can really break, for every night it returns anew with awe-inspiring completeness.

I became aware of the powerful atmosphere of the room. It is a perfectly normal and common experience for sensitive persons to become aware of the atmosphere of ancient houses, and my own experience began with something of this sort. The passage of time deepened it, enhanced the sense of immeasurable antiquity which environed me, and made me feel that the twentieth century was slipping away from under my feet. Yet, following my self-imposed resolve, I did not resist the feeling, instead I let it grow stronger.

A strange feeling that I was not alone began to creep insidiously over me. Under the cover of complete blackness, I felt that something animate and living was throbbing into existence. It was a vague feeling but a real one, and it was this, coupled with the increasing sense of the returning Past, that constituted my consciousness of something 'psychic'.

Yet nothing clear-cut, definite, emerged from this vague and general sense of an eerie life that pulsated through the darkness. The hours slipped on and, contrary to my expectation, the advancing night brought increasing coldness with it. The effects of the three-day fast which I had undertaken in order to increase my sensitivity, now showed themselves in growing chilliness. Cold air was creeping into the King's Chamber through the narrow ventilation shafts, and then creeping past the thin barrier of my light garment. My chilled flesh began to shiver under its thin shirt. I got up and dressed myself in the jacket which I had put off only a few hours before on account of the intense heat. Such is Eastern life at certain times of the year—tropical heat by day and a heavy fall of temperature by night.

To this day no one has discovered the mouths of these air channels on the outside of the Pyramid, although the approximate area of their positions is known. Some Egyptologists have even doubted whether the channels were ever carried right through to the outside, but the complete chilling of the air during my experience finally settles the point.

I sat down for the second time upon my stone seat and surrendered myself anew to the oppressive death-like silence, and to the all-prevailing sombre darkness of the chamber. With pliant soul I waited and wondered. For no reason at all I remembered irrelevantly that somewhere to the east the Suez Canal pursued its straight course through sand and marsh, and the stately Nile provided a backbone to this land.

The queer sepulchral stillness in the room, the empty stone coffin beside me, were not reassuring to one's nerves, while the break in my vigil seemed to have broken something else too, for very quickly I found that the sensing of invisible life around me rapidly rose into complete certainty. There *was* something throbbing and alive in my vicinity, although I could still see absolutely nothing. With this discovery the realization of my isolated and uncanny situation suddenly overwhelmed me. Here I was sitting alone in a queer room that was perched more than two hundred feet above the ground, high up above all the million people of Cairo, surrounded by total darkness, locked up and imprisoned in a strange building on the edge of a desert that stretched away for hundreds of miles, while outside this building—itself probably the oldest in the world—lay the grim tomb-cluttered necropolis of an ancient capital.

The great space of the King's Chamber became for me—who had investigated deeply into the psychic, into the mysteries of the occult, into the sorceries and wizardries of the Orient—peopled with unseen beings, with spirits who guarded this age-old building. One momentarily expected some ghostly voice to arise out of the all-embracing silence. I now thanked the early builders for those narrow vent-shafts which brought a steady but tiny supply of cool air into this hoary old room. That air travelled through nearly three hundred feet of the Pyramid before it arrived; no matter, it was still welcome. I am a man accustomed to solitude—indeed glad to enjoy it—but there was something uncanny and frightening in the solitude of this chamber.

The all-encompassing darkness began to press on my head like an iron weight. The shadow of uncalled-for fear flickered into me. I brushed it away immediately. To sit in the heart of this desert monument required no physical courage, but it did require some moral fortitude. No snakes were likely to emerge from holes or crevices, and no lawless wanderers were likely to climb its stepped sides and enter it at dead of night. Actually, the only signs of animal life I had seen came from a scared mouse which had met me early in the evening in the horizontal passage, and which had darted hither and thither between the creviceless granite walls in a frantic effort to escape out of reach of the dreaded beam of torchlight; from two incredibly aged yellowish-green lizards I had discovered clinging to the roof of the narrow cutting which extends inwards from the niche in the Queen's Chamber; and, lastly, from the bats in the subterranean vault. It was also true that a few crickets had chirped a good deal upon my entry into the Grand Gallery, but they had soon ceased. All that was over now, unbroken silence held the whole Pyramid as in a thrall. There was naught of a physical nature which could possibly injure one here, and yet—a vague uneasiness, a feeling that invisible eyes were watching me, recurred for the second time. The place possessed a dreamlike mysteriousness, a ghostly unreality. . . .

★　★　★

There are vibrations of force, sound and light which are beyond our normal range of detection. Laughing song and serious speech flash across the world to waiting wireless listeners, but they could never detect them were not their receiving sets properly tuned. I had now brought myself out of the state of mere receptive waiting into a forcefully concentrated condition of mind which focalized the whole of its attention upon an effort to pierce the black silence which surrounded it. If, in the result, my faculty of awareness was temporarily heightened to an abnormal extent by the intense inward concentration, who shall say that it is impossible I began to detect the presence of invisible forces?

I know only that as I 'tuned-in' by a method of interiorized attention which I had learnt long before this second visit to Egypt, I became aware that hostile forces had invaded the chamber. There was something abroad which I sensed as evil, dangerous. A nameless dread flickered into my heart and returned again and again soon after it was driven away.

I was still following my method of intense, single-pointed, inward-turned concentration, feeling followed its usual trend and changed into vision. Shadows began to flit to and fro in the shadowless room; gradually these took more definite shape, and malevolent countenances appeared suddenly quite close to my own face. Sinister images rose plainly before my mind's eye. Then a dark apparition advanced, looked at me with fixed sinister regard and raised its hands in a gesture of menace, as though seeking to inspire me with awe. Age-old spirits seemed to have crept out of the neighbouring necropolis, a necropolis so old that mummies had crumbled away inside their stone sarcophagi; the shades that clung to them made their unwelcome ascent to the place of my vigil. All the legends of evil ghosts who haunt the areas around the Pyramids, came back to memory with the same unpleasant detail with which they had been related by Arabs in the village not far off. When I had told a young Arab friend there of my intention to spend a night in the old building, he had tried to dissuade me.

'Every inch of ground is haunted,' had been his warning. 'There is an army of ghosts and genii in that territory.'

And now I could see that his warning was not a vain one. Spectral figures had begun to creep into and around the dark room wherein I sat, and the undefinable feeling of uneasiness which earlier had seized me was now receiving fit and full justification. Somewhere in the centre of that still thing which was my body, I knew that my heart beat like a hammer under the strain of it all. The dread of the supernatural, which lurks at the bottom of every human heart, touched me again. Fear, dread, horror persistently presented their evil visages to me in turn. Involuntarily my hands clenched themselves as tightly as a vice. But I was determined to go on, and although these phantom forms that moved across the room began by stirring in me a sense of alarm, they ended by provoking me to summon whatever reserves of courage and combativeness I could muster.

My eyes were closed and yet these grey, gliding, vaporous forms obtruded themselves across my vision. And always there came with them an implacable hostility, an ugly determination to deter me from my purpose.

A circle of antagonistic beings surrounded me. It would have been easy to end it all by switching on the light or by leaping up and dashing out of the chamber and running back a few hundred feet to the locked grille-entrance, where the armed guard would have provided gregarious comfort. It was an ordeal which imposed a subtle form of torture, that harried the soul and left the body untouched. Yet something inside me intimated just as implacably that I must see this thing through.

At last the climax came. Monstrous elemental creations, evil horrors of the underworld, forms of grotesque, insane, uncouth and fiendish aspect gathered around me and afflicted me with unimaginable repulsion. In a few minutes I lived through something which will leave a remembered record behind for all time. That incredible scene remains vividly photographed upon my memory. Never again would I repeat such an experiment; never again would I take up a nocturnal abode within the Great Pyramid.

The end came with startling suddenness. The malevolent ghostly invaders disappeared into the obscurity whence they had emerged, into the shadowy realms of the departed, taking with them their trail of noxious horrors. My half-shattered nerves experienced overwhelming relief such as a soldier feels when a fierce bombardment ends abruptly.

I do not know how long a period elapsed before I became conscious of a new presence in the chamber, of someone friendly and benevolent who stood at the entrance and looked down upon me with kindly eyes. With his arrival the atmosphere changed completely — and changed for the better. Something clean and sane had come with him. A new element began to play upon my overwrought sensitive being, soothing and calming it. He approached my stony seat, and I saw that he was followed by another figure. Both halted at my side and regarded me with grave looks, pregnant with prophetic meaning. I felt that some momentous hour of my life was at hand.

In my vision the apparition of these two beings presented an unforgettable picture. Their white robes, their sandalled feet, their wise aspect, their tall figures — all these return at once to the mind's eye. Withal they wore the unmistakable regalia of their office, High Priests of an ancient Egyptian cult. There was a light a-glimmer all around them, which in a most uncanny manner lit up the part of the room. Indeed, they looked more than men, bearing the bright mien of demi-gods; for their faces were set in unique cloistral calm.

They stood motionless as statues, regarding me, their hands crossed upon their breasts, remaining absolutely silent.

Was I functioning in some fourth dimension, aware and awake in some far-off epoch of the past? Had my sense of time regressed to the early days of Egypt? No; that could not be, for I perceived quickly that these two could see me and even now were about to address me.

The tall figures bent forward; the lips of one spirit seemed to move, his face close to mine, his eyes flashing spiritual fire, and his voice sounding in my ear.

'Why dost thou[1] come to this place, seeking to evoke the secret powers? Are not mortal ways enough for thee?' he asked.

I did not hear these words with any physical ear; certainly no sound-vibration disturbed the silence of the chamber. Yet I seemed to hear them much in the manner in which a deaf man, using an electric earphone, might hear the words sounding against his artificial ear-drum; but with this difference — that they were heard on the *inside* of the drum. Really, the voice which came to me might be termed a mental voice, because it was surely heard within my head, but that might give the wrong impression that it was a mere thought. Nothing could be farther from the truth. It *was* a voice.

And I answered: 'They are not!'

And he said: 'The stir of many crowds in the cities com-

[1]It would have been better for both writer and reader if this obsolete style of address were recast into modern form, but I prefer to let it stand as it came, even at the risk of provoking misunderstanding and derision. Any man would be justified, too, in doubting the possibility of an Egyptian spirit speaking English, and I might well doubt it with him, had I not heard the words myself. In any case, although these visions possess an authority which is sufficiently valid for me, and for those who trust me, I cannot and do not expect others to accept them so easily. For such events to happen in this prosaic twentieth century, for such spirit people to exist, is, of course, incredible.

forts the trembling heart of man. Go back, mingle with thy fellows, and thou wilt soon forget the light fancy that brings thee here.'

But I answered again: 'No, that cannot be.'

Still he strove once more.

'The way of Dream will draw thee far from the fold of reason. Some have gone upon it—and come back mad. Turn now, whilst there is yet time, and follow the path appointed for mortal feet.'

But I shook my head and muttered: 'I must follow this way. There is none other for me now.'

Then the priestly figure stepped forward closer and bent down again to where I sat.

I saw his aged face outlined by the surrounding darkness. He whispered against my ear: 'He who gains touch with us loses kin with the world. Art thou able to walk alone?'

I replied: 'I do not know.'

He whispered again: 'Come with me and then, when thou hast seen, answer again.'

And I saw, as in a far-off vision, a great city with a maze of streets. The picture approached rapidly until I noticed, close by, an old house that stood near a railed-in square. I saw a gloomy staircase that led up to a small garret on the top floor. My ghostly interlocutor appeared suddenly within the room, sitting by the bedside of an old man, whose matted hair and unkempt grey beard formed a fit frame for his rugged face. He must have long passed the evening of his life, for his ashen skin hung loosely upon the bones. His skinny, exhausted face drew my pity, but as I looked at him a chill came over me, for I saw his spirit struggling to leave its body, and in this ghostly battle there could be but one victor.

My guide gazed with pitying eyes at the figure in the bed. He held up his hands and said: 'A few more minutes, brother, and then thou shalt have peace. Behold, I have brought one who seeks the secret powers. Let thy last legacy be a few words to him.'

I suddenly became actor as well as witness in this strange scene.

With a croaking gasp that was terrible to hear, the dying man turned his head and looked me in the face. And though I wander to far Cathay, I shall never forget the brooding terror I saw in those eyes.

'You are younger than I,' he muttered. 'But I have wandered the world once, twice, three times. I, too, sought them—O! how I searched!' He halted for a minute, the while his head lay back on the pillow and he searched the pages of memory. Then he raised himself on his elbows, and stretched out a long thin arm. With its bony fingers and unyielding grip, his hand seemed like a skeleton's. He took my own and held my wrist like a vice; he peered into my eyes and I felt he was searching my soul.

'Fool! Fool!' he croaked, 'The only powers I found were the powers of the flesh and the devil. There are no other. They lie! Do you hear me?' he almost shouted, 'They lie!'

The effort was too much for him. He fell back upon his pillow—dead.

My guide made no comment, waiting for a full minute by the bedside. Then the vision was blotted out, I was back in the Pyramid once more.

He looked at me in silence, and I returned his glance with equal silence. He read my thought.

Out of the darkness came his last words: 'So be it. Thou hast chosen. Abide by thy choice for there is now no recall. Farewell,' and he was gone.

I was left alone with the other spirit, who so far had only played the part of a silent witness.

★　★　★

He moved closer so that he stood now in front of the marble coffer. His face revealed itself as the face of a man, very very old. I dared place no guess of years upon him.

'My son, the mighty lords of the secret powers have taken thee into their hands. Thou art to be led into the Hall of Learning tonight,' he explained dispassionately. 'Stretch thyself out upon this stone! In olden days it would have been within that yonder, upon a bed of papyrus-reeds,' and he pointed to the coffin-like sarcophagus.

It did not occur to me to do other than obey my mysterious visitant. I laid myself prone upon my back.

What happened immediately afterwards is still not very clear to me. It was as though he had unexpectedly given me a dose of some peculiar, slow-working anaesthetic, for all my muscles became taut, after which a paralyzing lethargy began to creep over my limbs. My entire body became heavy and numb. First, my feet became colder and colder. The feeling developed into a kind of iciness which moved by imperceptible degrees up my legs, reached the knees, whence it continued its mounting journey. It was as though I had sunk up to the waist in a pile of snow while on some mountain climb. All sensation in the lower limbs was numbed.

I appeared next to pass into a semi-somnolent condition and a mysterious intimation of approaching death crept into my mind. It did not trouble me, however, for I had long ago liberated myself from the ancient fear of death and arrived at a philosophic acceptance of its inevitability.

As this strange chilling sensation continued to grip me, to pass up my shivering spine, to overpower my entire body, I felt myself sinking inwards in consciousness to some central point within my brain, while my breathing became weaker and weaker.

When the chill reached my chest and the rest of my body was completely paralysed, something like a heart attack supervened, but it passed quickly and I knew that the supreme crisis was not far off.

Had I been able to move my stiff jaws, I might have laughed at the next thought which came to me. It was this: 'Tomorrow, they will find my dead body inside the Great Pyramid — and that will be the end of me.'

I was quite sure that all my sensations were due to the passage of my own spirit from physical life to the regions beyond death.

Although I knew perfectly well that I was passing through all the sensations of dying, all opposition had now vanished.

At last, my concentrated consciousness lay in the head alone, and there was a final mad whirl within my brain. I had the sensation of being caught up in a tropical whirlwind and seemed to pass upwards through a narrow hole; then there was a momentary dread of being launched in infinite space, I leapt into the unknown — and I was *Free*!

No other word will express the delightful sense of liberation which then became mine. I had changed into a mental being, a creature of thought and feeling yet without the clogging handicap of the heavy flesh body in which I had been shut up. I had gone ghost-like clean out of my earthly body, like a dead man rising out of his tomb, but had certainly gone into no sort of unconsciousness. My sense of existence in fact, was intensely more vivid than before. Above all, with this exodus to a higher dimension, I felt *free*, blissfully, languorously free, in this fourth dimension to which I had penetrated.

At first I found myself lying on my back, as horizontal as the body I had just vacated, floating above the stone floor block. Then came a sensation of some invisible hand turning me upright on my heels, after pushing me forward a little, and placing me properly on my feet. Ultimately, I had a curiously combined feeling of both standing and floating simultaneously.

I gazed down upon the deserted body of flesh and bone, which was lying prone and motionless on the stone block. The inexpressive face was upturned, the eyes were scarcely open, yet the pupils gleamed sufficiently to indicate that the lids were not really closed. The arms were folded across the breast — certainly not an attitude which I could remember having assumed. Had someone crossed those hands without my being aware of the movement? The legs and feet were stretched out side by side, touching each other. There lay the seemingly dead form of myself, the form from which I had withdrawn.

I noted a trail of faint silvery light projecting itself down from me, the new *me*, to the cataleptic creature who lay upon the block. This was surprising, but more surprising still was my discovery that this mysterious psychic umbilical cord was contributing towards the illumination of the corner of the King's Chamber where I hovered; showing up the wall-stones in a soft moonbeam-like light.

I was but a phantom, a bodiless creature sojourning in space. I knew, at last, why those wise Egyptians of old had given, in their hieroglyphs, the pictured symbol of the bird to man's soul-form. I had experienced a sense of increased height and breadth, a spreading out just as though I had a pair of wings. Had I not risen into the air and remained floating above my discarded body, even as a bird rises into the sky and remains circling around a point? Did I not have the sensation of being environed by a great void? Yes, the bird symbol was a true one.

Yes; I had risen into space, disentangled my soul from its mortal skein, separated myself into two twin parts, left the world which I had known so long. I experienced a sense of being etherealized, of intense lightness, in this duplicate body which I now inhabited. As I gazed down at the cold stone block upon which my body lay, a single idea obtained recognition in my mind, a single realization overwhelmed me. It expressed itself to me in a few brief, silent words: *'This is the state of death. Now I know that I am a soul, that I can exist apart from the body. I shall always believe that, for I have proved it.'*

This notion clutched hold of me with an iron grip, the while I was poised lightly above my empty flesh tenement. I had proved survival in what I thought the most satisfactory way — by actually dying and then surviving! I kept on looking at the recumbent relic which I had left behind. Somehow, it fascinated me. Was that discarded form the thing which, for so many years, I had considered as myself? I perceived then, with complete clarity, that it was nothing more than a mass of unintelligent, unconscious, fleshly matter. As I regarded those unseeing unresponsive eyes, the irony of the whole situation struck me forcibly. My earthly body had really imprisoned me, the real 'me', but now I was free. I had been borne hither and thither upon this planet by an organism which I had long confused with my real central self.

The sense of gravity seemed to have gone, and I was literally floating on air, with that strange half-suspended, half-standing feeling.

Suddenly, by my side, appeared the old priest, grave and imperturbable. With upturned eyes, his face more ennobled still, with reverent mood, he prayed: 'O Amen, O Amen, who art in Heaven, turn thy face upon the dead body of thy son, and make him well in the spirit-world. It is finished.' And then he addressed me: 'Thou hast now learned the great lesson. *Man, whose soul was born out of the Undying, can never really die.* Set down this truth in words known to men. Behold!'

And out of space there came the half-remembered face of a woman whose funeral I had attended more than twenty years before; then the familiar countenance of a man who had been more than a friend and whom I had last seen laid to rest in his coffin twelve years previously; and, finally, the sweet smiling picture of a child I knew who had died in an accidental fall.

These three peered at me with tranquil faces, and their friendly voices sounded once again around me. I had the shortest of conversations with the so-called dead, who soon melted away and vanished.

'They too live, even as thou livest, even as this Pyramid which has seen the death of half a world, lives on,' said the High Priest.

'Know, my son, that in this ancient fane lies the lost record of the early races of man and of the Covenant which they made with their Creator through the first of His great prophets. Know, too, that chosen men were brought here of old to be shown this Covenant that they might return to their fellows and keep the great secret alive. Take back with thee the warning that when men forsake their Creator and look on their fellows with hate, as with the princes of Atlantis in whose time this Pyramid was built, they are destroyed by the weight of their own iniquity, even as the people of Atlantis were destroyed.

'It is not the Creator who sank Atlantis, but the selfishness, the cruelty, the spiritual blindness of the people who dwelt on those doomed islands. The Creator loves all; but the lives of men are governed by invisible laws which He has set over them. Take back this warning, then.'

There surged up in me a great desire to see this mysterious Covenant and the spirit must have read my thought, for he quickly said: 'To all things there is an hour. Not yet, my son, not yet.'

I was disappointed.

He looked at me for a few seconds.

'No man of thy people hath yet been permitted to behold such a thing, but because thou art a man versed in these things, and hast come among us bearing goodwill and understanding in thy heart, some satisfaction thou shalt have. Come with me!'

And then a strange thing happened. I seemed to fall into a kind of semi-coma, my consciousness was momentarily blotted out, and the next thing I knew was that I had been transported to another place. I found myself in a long passage which was softly lit, although no lamp or window was visible; I fancied that the illumination was none other than the halo-like emanation around my companion combined with the radiation from the luminous cord of ether which extended behind me, yet I realized that these would not sufficiently explain it. The walls were built up with a glowing pinkish terracotta coloured stone, slabbed with the thinnest of joints. The floor sloped downwards at precisely the same angle as the Pyramid entrance itself descends. The masonry was well finished. The passage was square and fairly low, but not uncomfortably so. I could not find the source of its mysterious illuminant, yet the interior was bright as though a lamp were playing on it.[1]

[1]Dr Abbate Pacha, Vice-President of the Institut Egyptien, spent a night in the desert near the Pyramids, together with Mr William Groff, a member of the Institut. In the official report of their experiences, the latter said: 'Towards eight o'clock, in the evening, I noticed a light which appeared to turn slowly around the Third Pyramid almost up to the apex; it was like a small flame. The light made three circuits round the Pyramid and then disappeared. For a good part of the night I attentively watched this Pyramid; towards eleven o'clock I again noticed the same light, but this time it was of a bluish colour; it mounted slowly almost in a straight line and arrived at a certain height above the Pyramid's summit and then disappeared.' By pursuing enquiries among the Bedouins, Mr Groff discovered that this mysterious light had been seen more or less frequently in the past, the traditions of its existence stretching back centuries. The Arabs put it down to guardian-spirits of the Pyramid, but Groff tried to find a natural explanation for it, though without success.

The High Priest bade me follow him a little way down the passage. 'Look not backwards,' he warned me, 'nor turn thy head.' We passed some distance down the incline and I saw a large temple-like chamber opening out of the farther end. I knew perfectly well that I was inside or below the Pyramid, but I had never seen such a passage or chamber before. Evidently they were secret and had defied discovery until this day. I could not help feeling tremendously excited about this startling find, and an equally tremendous curiosity seized me as to where and what the entrance was. Finally, I *had* to turn my head and take a swift look backwards at what I hoped was the secret door. I had entered the place by no visible entrance, but at the farther end I saw that what should have been an opening was closed with square blocks and apparently cemented. I found myself gazing at a blank wall; then, as swiftly whirled away by some irresistible force until the whole scene was blotted out and I had floated off into space again. I heard the words: 'Not yet, not yet,' repeated as in an echo and a few moments later saw my inert unconscious body lying on the stone.

'My son,' came a murmur from the High Priest, 'It matters not whether thou discoverest the door or not. Find but the secret passage within the mind that will lead thee to the hidden chamber within thine own soul, and thou shalt have found something worthy indeed. Thy mystery of the Great Pyramid is the mystery of thine own self. The secret chambers and ancient records are all contained in thine own nature. The lesson of the Pyramid is that man must turn inward, must venture to the unknown centre of his being to find his soul, even as he must venture to the unknown depths of this fane to find its profoundest secret. Farewell!'

My mind whirled into some vortex that caught me; I slipped helplessly, sucked downwards, ever downwards; heavy torpor overcame me, and I seemed to melt back into my physical body; I strained my will, pushing and trying to move its rigid muscles, but failed and finally I swooned...

I opened my eyes with a shock, in inky blackness. When the numbness passed, my hands groped for the torch and switched the light on. I was back in the King's Chamber, still tremendously excited, so excited in fact, that I jumped up and shouted, my voice echoing back in muffled tones. But, instead of feeling the floor beneath my feet, I found myself falling through space. Only by throwing both hands on the edge of the stone block and clinging to the sides did I save myself. I then realized what had happened. In rising I had unwittingly moved to the far end of the block and my feet were now dangling over the excavated hole in the north-west corner of the floor.

I picked myself up and got back to safety, secured the lamp and threw a beam of light upon my watch. The glass was cracked in two places, where I had struck my hand and wrist against the wall in jumping up, but the works still ticked mer-rily away; and then, as I noted the time, I almost laughed outright despite the solemnity of my surroundings.

For it was precisely the melodramatic hour of midnight, both hands pointing to twelve, neither more or less!

★ ★ ★

When the armed police guard unlocked the iron grille soon after dawn, a dusty, weary, tired-eyed figure stumbled out of the Great Pyramid's dark entrance. He made his way down the large square blocks of stone into the early morning sun-light and gazed, with eyes that blinked, at the flat, familiar landscape. His first act was to take several deep breaths, one after the other. Then he instinctively turned his face upwards towards Ra, the sun, and silently thanked him for this blessed gift of light to mankind.

2

MEETINGS WITH INDIAN SAGES: SRI SANKARACHARYA AND SRI RAMANA MAHARSHI

From *A Search in Secret India* (London: Rider & Co., 1935), pp. 126, 128-31, 301-10. (In USA: 1st edn. rev., York Beach, ME: Samuel Weiser, 1985. Copyright 1985 Kenneth T. Hurst.) Used by permission of the publisher and Mr Hurst.

SRI SANKARACHARYA

While in Chingleput, Paul Brunton has the opportunity of an interview with the spiritual head of South India, Sri Shankaracharya of Kumbakonam (or Kamakoti), who holds the office founded by the great Sankara of the eighth century, CE.

I look at him in silence. This short man is clad in the ochre-coloured robe of a monk and leans his weight on a friar's staff. I have been told that he is on the right side of forty, hence I am surprised to find his hair quite grey.

His noble face, pictured in grey and brown, takes an honoured place in the long portrait gallery of my memory. That elusive element which the French aptly term *spirituel* is present in this face. His expression is modest and mild, the large dark eyes being extraordinarily tranquil and beautiful. The nose is short, straight and classically regular. There is a rugged little beard on his chin, and the gravity of his mouth is most noticeable. Such a face might have belonged to one of the saints who graced the Christian Church during the Middle Ages, except that this one possesses the added quality of intellectuality. I suppose we of the practical West would say that he has the eyes of a dreamer. Somehow, I feel in an inexplicable way that there is something more than mere dreams behind those heavy lids.

'Your Holiness has been very kind to receive me,' I remark, by way of introduction.

He turns to my companion, the writer, and says something in the vernacular. I guess its meaning correctly.

'His Holiness understands your English, but he is too afraid that you will not understand his own. So he prefers to have me translate his answers,' says Venkataramani.

I shall sweep through the earlier phases of this interview, because they are more concerned with myself than with this Hindu Primate. He asks about my personal experiences in the country; he is very interested in ascertaining the exact impressions which Indian people and institutions make upon a foreigner. I give him my candid impressions, mixing praise and criticism freely and frankly.

★ ★ ★

I am quick to notice that Sri Shankara does not decry the West in order to exalt the East, as so many in his land do. He admits that each half of the globe possesses its own set of virtues and vices, and that in this way they are roughly equal! He hopes that a wiser generation will fuse the best points of Asiatic and European civilizations into a higher and balanced social scheme.

I drop the subject and ask permission for some personal questions. It is granted without difficulty.

'How long has Your Holiness held this title?'

'Since 1907. At that time I was only twelve years old. Four years after my appointment I retired to a village on the banks of the Cauvery, where I gave myself up to meditation and study for three years. Then only did my public work begin.'

'You rarely remain at your headquarters in Kumbakonam I take it?'

'The reason for that is that I was invited by the Maharajah of Nepal in 1918 to be his guest for a while. I accepted and since then have been travelling slowly towards his state in the far north. But see! — during all those years I have not been able to advance more than a few hundred miles, because the tradition of my office requires that I stay in every vil-

lage and town which I pass on the route or which invites
me, if it is not too far off. I must give a spiritual discourse
in the local temple and some teaching to the inhabitants.'

I broach the matter of my quest and His Holiness questions me about the different Yogis or holy men I have so
far met. After that, I frankly tell him: 'I would like to meet
someone who has high attainments in Yoga and can give
some sort of proof or demonstration of them. There are
many of your holy men who can only give one more talk
when they are asked for this proof. Am I asking too much?'

The tranquil eyes meet mine.

There is a pause for a whole minute. His Holiness fingers
his beard.

'If you are seeking initiation into real Yoga of the higher
kind, then you are not seeking too much. Your earnestness
will help you, while I can perceive the strength of your determination; but a light is beginning to awaken within you
which will guide you to what you want, without doubt.'

I am not sure whether I correctly understand him.

'So far I have depended on myself for guidance. Even some
of your ancient sages say that there is no other god than that
which is within ourselves,' I hazard.

And the answer swiftly comes: 'God is everywhere. How
can one limit Him to one's own self? He supports the entire
universe.'

I feel that I am getting out of my depth and immediately
turn the talk away from this semi-theological strain.

'What is the most practical course for me to take?'

'Go on with your travels. When you have finished them,
think of various Yogis and holy men you have met; then pick
out the one who makes the most appeal to you. Return to
him, and he will surely bestow his initiation upon you.'

I look at his calm profile and admire its singular serenity.

'But suppose, Your Holiness, that none of them makes
sufficient appeal to me. What then?'

'In that case you will have to go on alone until God Himself initiates you. Practise meditation regularly; contemplate
the higher things with love in your heart; think often of the
soul and that will help to bring you to it. The best time to

practise is the hour of waking; the next best time is the hour of twilight. The world is calmer at those times and will disturb your meditation less.'

He gazes benevolently at me. I began to envy the saintly peace which dwells on his bearded face. Surely, his heart has never known the devastating upheavals which have scarred mine? I am stirred to ask him impulsively: 'If I fail, may I then turn to you for assistance?'

Sri Shankara gently shakes his head.

'I am the head of a public institution, a man whose time no longer belongs to himself. My activities demand almost all my time. For years I have spent only three hours in sleep each night. How can I take personal pupils? You must find a master who devotes his time to them.'

'But I am told that real masters are rare, and that a European is unlikely to find them.'

He nods his assent to my statement, but adds: 'Truth exists. It can be found.'

'Can you not direct me to such a master, one who you know is competent to give me proofs of the reality of higher Yoga?'

His Holiness does not reply till after an interval of protracted silence.

'Yes. I know of only two masters in India who could give you what you wish. One of them lives in Benares, hidden away in a large house, which is itself hidden among spacious grounds. Few people are permitted to obtain access to him; certainly, no European has yet been able to intrude upon his seclusion. I could send you to him, but I fear that he may refuse to admit a European.'

'And the other——?' My interest is strangely stirred.

'The other man lives in the interior, farther south. I visited him once and know him to be a high master. I recommend that you go to him.'

'Who is he?'

'He is called the Maharishee.[1] His abode is on

---

[1] The title is derived from Sanskrit. *Maha* means great: *Rishee* means sage or seer. Hence, the Great Sage.

Arunachala, the Mountain of the Holy Beacon, which is in the territory of North Arcot. Shall I provide you with full instructions, so that you may discover him?'

A picture flashes suddenly before my mind's eye.

I see the yellow-robed friar, who has vainly persuaded me to accompany him to his teacher. I hear him murmuring the name of a hill. It is: 'The Hill of the Holy Beacon.'

'Many thanks, Your Holiness,' I rejoin, 'but I have a guide who comes from the place.'

'Then you will go there?'

I hesitate.

'All arrangements have been made for my departure from the South tomorrow,' I mutter uncertainly.

'In that case I have a request to make.'

'With pleasure.'

'Promise me that you will not leave South India before you have met the Maharishee.'

I read in his eyes a sincere desire to help me. The promise is given.

A benignant smile crosses his face.

'Do not be anxious. You shall discover that which you seek.'

A murmur from the crowd which is in the street penetrates the house.

'I have taken up too much of your valuable time,' I apologize. 'I am indeed sorry.'

Sri Shankara's grave mouth relaxes. He follows me into the ante-room and whispers something into the ear of my companion. I catch my name in the sentence.

At the door I turn to bow in farewell salutation. His Holiness calls me back to receive a parting message: 'You shall always remember me, and I shall always remember you!'

SRI RAMANA MAHARSHI

Meditating under the guidance of the sage in his remote jungle hermitage, Paul Brunton experiences samadhi, and returns with a message for mankind.

My pen would wander on into some account of scenic life

around me, and into further record of many talks with the Maharishee, but it is now time to draw this chronicle to a close.

I study him intently and gradually come to see in him the child of a remote Past, when the discovery of spiritual truth was reckoned of no less value than is the discovery of a gold mine today. It dawns upon me with increasing force that in this quiet and obscure corner of South India, I have been led to one of the last of India's spiritual supermen. The serene figure of this living sage brings the legendary figures of his country's ancient Rishees nearer to me. One senses that the most wonderful part of this man is withheld. His deepest soul, which one instinctively recognizes as being loaded with rich wisdom, eludes one. At times he still remains curiously aloof, and at other times the kindly benediction of his interior grace binds me to him with hoops of steel. I learn to submit to the enigma of his personality, and to accept him as I find him. But if, humanly speaking, he is well insulated against outside contacts, whoever discovers the requisite Ariadne's thread can walk the inner path leading to spiritual contact with him. And I like him greatly because he is so simple and modest, when an atmosphere of authentic greatness lies so palpably around him; because he makes no claims to occult powers and hierophantic knowledge to impress the mystery-loving nature of his countrymen; and because he is so totally without any traces of pretension that he strongly resists every effort to canonize him during his lifetime.

It seems to me that the presence of men like Maharishee ensures the continuity down history of a divine message from regions not easily accessible to us all. It seems to me, further, that one must accept the fact that such a sage comes to reveal something to us, not to argue anything with us. At any rate, his teachings make a strong appeal to me for his personal attitude and practical method, when understood, are quite scientific in their way. He brings in no supernatural power and demands no blind religious faith. The sublime spirituality of the Maharishee's atmosphere and the rational self-questioning of his philosophy find but a faint echo in yonder temple. Even the word 'God' is rarely on his lips. He avoids the dark and debatable waters of wizardry, in which so many promising voyages have ended in shipwreck. He simply puts forward a way of self-analysis, which can be practised irrespective of any ancient or modern theories and beliefs which one may hold, a way that will finally lead man to true self-understanding.

I follow this process of self-divestment in the effort to arrive at pure integral being. Again and again I am aware that the Maharishee's mind is imparting something to my own, though no words may be passing between us. The shadow of impending departure hangs over my efforts, yet I spin out my stay until bad health takes a renewed hand in the game and accelerates an irrevocable decision to go. Indeed, out of the deep inner urgency which drew me here has come enough will power to overthrow the plaints of a tired sick body and weary brain and to enable me to maintain residence in this hot static air. But Nature will not be defeated for long and before long a physical breakdown becomes threateningly imminent. Spiritually my life is nearing its peak, but—strange paradox!—physically it is slipping downwards to a point lower than it has hitherto touched. For a few hours before the arrival of the culminating experience of my contact with the Maharishee, I start to shiver violently and to perspire with abnormal profuseness—intimations of coming fever.

I return hastily from an exploration of some usually veiled sanctuaries of the great temple and enter the hall when the evening meditation period has run out half its life. I slip quietly to the floor and straightaway assume my regular meditation posture. In a few seconds I compose myself and bring all wandering thoughts to a strong centre. An intense interiorization of consciousness comes with the closing of eyes.

The Maharishee's seated form floats in a vivid manner before my mind's eye. Following his frequently repeated instruction I endeavour to pierce through the mental picture into that which is formless, his real being and inner nature, his soul. To my surprise the effort meets with almost instantaneous success and the picture disappears again, leaving me with nothing more than a strongly felt sense of his intimate presence.

The mental questionings which have marked most of my earlier meditations have lately begun to cease. I have repeatedly interrogated my consciousness of physical, emotional and mental sensations in turn, but, dissatisfied in the quest of self, have eventually left them all. I have then applied the attention of consciousness to its own centre, striving to become aware of its place of origin. Now comes the supreme moment. In that concentration of stillness, the mind withdrawn into itself, one's familiar world begins to fade off in shadowy vagueness. One is apparently environed for a while by sheer nothingness, having arrived at a kind of mental blank wall. And one has to be as intense as possible to maintain one's fixed attention. But how hard to leave the lazy dalliance of our surface life and draw the mind inwards to a pin-point of concentration!

Tonight I flash swiftly to this point, with barely a skirmish against the continuous sequence of thoughts which usually play the prelude to its arrival. Some new and powerful force comes into dynamic action within my inner world and bears me inwards with resistless speed. The first great battle is over, almost without a stroke, and a pleasurable, happy, easeful feeling succeeds its high tension.

In the next stage I stand apart from the intellect, conscious that it is thinking, but warned by an intuitive voice that it is merely an instrument. I watch these thoughts with a weird detachment. The power to think, which has hitherto been a matter for merely ordinary pride, now becomes a thing from which to escape, for I perceive with startling clarity that I have been its unconscious captive. There follows the sudden desire to stand outside the intellect and just *be*. I want to dive into a place deeper than thought. I want to know what it will feel like to deliver myself from the constant bondage of the brain, but to do so with all my attention awake and altert.

It is strange enough to be able to stand aside and watch the very action of the brain as though it were someone else's, and to see how thoughts take their rise and then die, but it is stranger still to realize intuitively that one is about to penetrate into the mysteries which hide the innermost recesses of man's soul. I feel like some Columbus about to land on an uncharted continent. A perfectly controlled and subdued anticipation quietly thrills me.

But how to divorce oneself from the age-old tyranny of thoughts? I remember that the Maharishee has never suggested that I should attempt to force the stoppage of thinking. 'Trace thought to its place of origin,' is his reiterated counsel, 'watch for the real self to reveal itself, and then your thoughts will die down of their own accord.' So, feeling that I have found the birthplace of thinking, I let go of the powerfully positive attitude which has brought my attention to this point and surrender myself to complete passivity, yet still keeping as intently watchful as a snake of its prey.

This poised condition reigns until I discover the correctness of the sage's prophecy. The waves of thought naturally begin to diminish. The workings of logical rational sense drop towards zero point. The strangest sensation I have experienced till now grips me. Time seems to reel dizzily as the antennae of my rapidly growing intuition begin to reach out into the unknown. The reports of my bodily senses are no longer heard, felt, remembered. I know that at any moment I shall be standing *outside* things, on the very edge of the world's secret...

Finally it happens. Thought is extinguished like a snuffed candle. The intellect withdraws into its real ground, that is, consciousness working unhindered by thoughts. I perceive, what I have suspected for some time and what the Maharishee has confidently affirmed, that the mind takes its rise in a transcendental source. The brain has passed into a state of complete suspension, as it does in deep sleep, yet there is not the slightest loss of consciousness. I remain perfectly calm and fully aware of who I am and what is occurring. Yet my sense of awareness has been drawn out of the narrow confines of the separate personality; it has turned into something sublimely all-embracing. Self still exists, but it is a changed, radiant self. For something that is far superior to the unimportant personality which *was* I, some deeper, diviner being rises into consciousness and *becomes* me. With it arrives an amazing new sense of absolute freedom, for thought is like a loom-shuttle which is always going to and fro, and to be freed from its tyrannical motion is to step out of prison into the open air.

I find myself outside the rim of world consciousness. The planet which has so far harboured me, disappears. I am in the midst of an ocean of blazing light. The latter, I feel rather than think, is the primeval stuff out of which worlds are created, the first state of matter. It stretches away into untellable infinite space, incredibly *alive*.

I touch, as in a flash, the meaning of this mysterious universal drama which is being enacted in space, and then return to the primal point of my being. I, the new I, rest in the lap of holy bliss. I have drunk the Platonic Cup of Lethe, so that yesterday's bitter memories and tomorrow's anxious cares have disappeared completely. I have attained a divine liberty and an almost indescribable felicity. My arms embrace all creation with profound sympathy, for I understand in the deepest possible way that to know all is not merely to pardon all, but to love all. My heart is remoulded in rapture.

How shall I record these experiences through which I next pass, when they are too delicate for the touch of my pen? Yet the starry truths which I learn may be translated into the language of earth, and the effort will not be a vain one. So I seek, all too roughly, to bring back some memorials of the wonderful archaic world which stretches out, untracked and unpathed, behind the human mind.

* * *

- Man is grandly related and a greater Being suckled him than his mother. In his wiser moments he may come to know this.

- Once, in the far days of his own past, man took an oath of lofty allegiance and walked, turbaned in divine grandeur, with the gods. If today the busy world calls to him with imperious demand and he gives himself up to it, there are those who have not forgotten his oath and he shall be reminded of it at the appropriate hour.

● There is That in man which belongs to an imperishable race. He neglects his true self almost completely, but his neglect can never affect or alter its shining greatness. He may forget it and entirely go to sleep in the senses, yet on the day when it stretches forth its hand and touches him, he shall remember who he is and recover his soul.

● Man does not put the true value upon himself because he has lost the divine sense. Therefore he runs after another man's opinion, when he could find complete certitude more surely in the spiritually authoritative centre of his own being. The Sphinx surveys no earthly landscape. Its unflinching gaze is always directed inwards, and the secret of its inscrutable smile is self-knowledge.

● He who looks within himself and perceives only discontent, frailty, darkness and fear, need not curl his lip in mocking doubt. Let him look deeper and longer, deeper and longer, until he presently becomes aware of faint tokens and breath-like indications which appear when the heart is still. Let him heed them well, for they will take life and grow into high thoughts that will cross the threshold of his mind like wandering angels, and these again shall become forerunners of a voice which will come later — the voice of a hidden, recondite and mysterious being who inhabits his centre, who is his own ancient self.

● The divine nature reveals itself anew in every human life, but if a man walk indifferently by, then the revelation is as seed on stony ground. No one is excluded from this divine consciousness; it is man who excludes himself. Men make formal and pretentious enquiry into the mystery and meaning of life, when all the while each bird perched upon a green bough, each child holding its fond mother's hand, has solved the riddle and carries the answer in its face. That Life which brought you to birth, O Man! is nobler and greater than your farthest thought; believe in its beneficent intention towards you and obey its subtle injunctions whispered to your heart in half-felt intuitions.

● The man who thinks he may live as freely as his unconsidered desires prompt him and yet not carry the burden of an eventual reckoning, is binding his life to a hollow dream. Whoever sins against his fellows or against himself pronounces his own sentence thereby. He may hide his sins from the sight of others, but he cannot hide them from the all-recording eyes of the gods. Justice still rules the world with inexorable weight, though its operations are often unseen and though it is not always to be found in stone-built courts of law. Whoever escapes from paying the legal penalties of earth can never escape from paying the just penalties which the gods impose. Nemesis —remorseless and implacable—holds such a man in jeopardy every hour.

● Those who have been held under the bitter waters of sorrow, those who have moved through shadowed years in the midst of tears, will be somewhat readier to receive the truth which life is ever silently voicing. If they can perceive nothing else, they can perceive the tragical transience which attends the smiles of fortune. Those who refuse to be deluded by their brighter hours will not suffer so greatly from their darker ones. There is no life that is not made up of the warp of pleasure and the woof of suffering. Therefore no man can afford to walk with proud and pontifical air. He who does so takes his perambulation at a grave peril. For humility is the only befitting robe to wear in the presence of the unseen gods, who may remove in a few days what has been acquired during many years. The fate of all things moves in cycles and only the thoughtless observer can fail to note this fact. Even in the universe it may be seen that every perihelion is succeeded by an aphelion. So in the life and fortunes of man, the flood of prosperity may be succeeded by the ebb of privation, health may be a fickle guest, while love may come only to wander again. But when the night of protracted agony dies, the dawn of new-found wisdom glimmers. The last lesson of these things is that the eternal refuge in man, unnoticed and unsought as it may be, must become what it was once—his solace, or disappointment and suffering will periodically conspire to drive him in upon it. No man is so lucky that the gods permit him to avoid these two great tutors of the race.

● A man will feel safe, protected, secure, only when he discovers that the radiant wings of sublimity enfold him. While he persists in remaining unillumined his best inventions shall become his worst impediments, and everything that draws him closer to the material frame of things shall become another knot he must later untie. For he is inseparably allied to his ancient past, he stands always in the presence of his inner divinity and cannot shake it off. Let him, then, not remain unwitting of this fact but deliver himself, his wordly cares and secret burdens, into the beautiful care of his better self and it shall not fail him. Let him do this, if he would live with gracious peace and die with fearless dignity.

● He who has once seen his real self will never again hate another. There is no sin greater than hatred, no sorrow worse than the legacy of lands splashed with blood which it inevitably bestows, no result more certain than that it will recoil on those who send it forth. Though none can hope to pass beyond their sight, the gods themselves stand unseen as silent witnesses of man's awful handiwork. A moaning world lies in woe all around them, yet sublime peace is close at hand for all; weary men, tried by sorrow and torn by doubts, stumble and grope their way through the darkened streets of life, yet a great light beats down upon the paving-stones before them. Hate will pass from the world only when man learns to see the faces of his fellows, not merely by the ordinary light of day, but by the transfiguring light of their divine possibilities; when he can regard them with the reverence they deserve as the faces of beings in whose hearts dwells an element akin to that Power which men name God.

● All that is truly grand in Nature and inspiringly beautiful in the arts speaks to man of himself. Where the priest has failed his people the illumined artist takes up his forgotten message and procures hints of the soul for them. Whoever can recall rare moments when beauty made him a dweller amid the eternities should, whenever the world tires him, turn memory into a spur and seek out the sanctuary within. Thither he should wander for a little peace, a flush of strength and a glimmer of light, confident that the moment he succeeds in touching his true selfhood he will draw infinite support and find perfect compensation. Scholars may burrow like moles among the growing piles of modern books and ancient manuscripts which line the walls of the house of learning, but they can learn no deeper secret than this, no higher truth than the supreme truth that man's very self is divine. The wistful hopes of man may wane as the years pass, but the hope of undying life, the hope of perfect love, and the hope of assured happiness, shall ultimately find a certain fulfilment; for they constitute prophetic instincts of an ineluctable destiny which can in no way be avoided.

● The world looks to ancient prophets for its finest thoughts and cringes before dusty eras for its noblest ethics. But when a man receives the august revelation of his own starry nature, he is overwhelmed. All that is worthy in thought and feeling now comes unsought to his feet. Inside the cloistral quiet of his mind arise visions not less sacred than those of the Hebrew and Arab seers, who reminded their race of its divine source. By this same auroral light Buddha understood and brought news of Nirvana to men. And such is the all-embracing love which this understanding awakens, that Mary Magdalene wept out her soiled life at the feet of Jesus.

● No dust can ever settle on the grave grandeur of these ancient truths, though they have lain in time since the early days of our race. No people has ever existed but has also received intimations of this deeper life which is open to man. Whoever is ready to accept them must not only apprehend these truths with his intelligence, until they sparkle among his thoughts like stars among the asteroids, but must appropriate them with his heart until they inspire him to diviner action.

3

THE OVERSELF IN ACTION

From *The Quest of the Overself* (London: Rider & Co., 1937), pp. 264-73. (In USA: 2nd edn. rev., York Beach, ME: Samuel Weiser, 1984. Copyright 1984 by Kenneth T. Hurst.) Used by permission of the publisher and Mr Hurst.

This Secret Path is not alone a path of mind; it may, and should, easily become the forerunner of a path of outer achievement, the more dynamic because it is the more inspired. *Its object is not to withdraw men into monastic idleness but to help them work more wisely and more effectively in their own spheres of usefulness.*

In general it may be said that the man who has become sufficiently advanced upon this path will sooner or later build for himself an environment that is entirely congenial and will enter into a domain of worldly activity that will be pleasant to his higher outlook; such will be the external recoil to his inner mental creation.

There are exceptions to this general principle and they are constituted by those cases where men, as an act of deliberate self-surrender, enter fearlessly into uncongenial or even hostile environments as a voluntary service to others or at a diviner bidding. In a sense these men are really martyrs, but the surrender of their ego-will to the divine will of the Overself has removed the worst part of their martyrdom. They will expect no return for such service, they will ask for no tangible recompense or expressed gratitude.

We Westerners detest and distrust the philosophic conceptions which would appear to lead us away from the busy world into an 'unreal' cloudy realm. We believe and can only believe in creeds that sanctify the strenuous life. We are undoubtedly right. Yet a path is available which gives us the best of both worlds.

The concentrative power developed by a man during this daily practice will serve him equally well in the sphere of active existence. Whatever he undertakes will be marked by a more purposeful attention. For instance, his dealings with others will become more direct and fruitful to both sides and he will come far more quickly to the point in conversation. In short, a new element, a kind of higher practicality, will show itself in small matters as well as in the most important. He will always carry out with the utmost carefulness, devoted faithfulness and highest integrity whatever duty is entrusted to him by the combined forces of fate and the Overself.

Psychologically, the effects of right meditation practice will show themselves in a better quality of thinking, in greater depth of concentrative power, and in a general clarification of the mind. The principles underlying any subject or situation will be quickly grasped, when others are still studying the details.

A man who has made sufficient progress in these practices to obtain some degree of mental control, some closer feeling of the existence of the Overself, need not fear overmuch the materializing effect of continuous activity. He will illustrate repose in the midst of activity. While his mind rests in a more or less abiding calm, his brain, hands and feet may indeed be busy with the active affairs of every day. While his inner life flows gently and happily like a placid stream through English meadows, his external life may be undergoing violent storms. The value of such a balanced inner life in our unsettled age is beyond price. Such a man will demonstrate, however imperfectly, that the association of sublime inspiration with positive action is a perfectly possible combination. All days then become holy days. When the Overself thus goes into action, the meanest life is made sacred. The perfume of divinity is sprayed over the petty incidents of every day and glorifies them.

An extraordinary and indescribable inner peace will live within him. It will be his place of anchorage in a disorderly epoch when nothing else seems either secure or stable. He will thus move calmly on his road, his feet planted firmly at every step, where others rush wildly to and fro under the stress of twentieth-century convulsion. He will work with that spirit of gentle unhurriedness allied with exacting efficiency which is such a marked characteristic of the successful Japanese. The sublime serenity of the Overself seems remote indeed from the harsh rumble of New York's elevated railroad, from the ever-purring motor traffic of the Champs-Elysées, and from the teeming throngs of London's Strand—nevertheless, even amid such environments, he will possess it!

Thus, living as close to the Divine Centre as he can, he may still be able to take his appropriate place in the world, no longer as its slave, but as Nature's co-operator. While his inmost being dwells in a strange spirituality, he himself will be able to move in the very midst of stress and tumult, not blind to its existence or indifferent to its problems, but nevertheless inwardly poised and untroubled. Therefore he can cope more effectively with these problems. He has found that at the centre—whether of self or the universe—there dwells real safety and sanity.

All these effects will be brought about whether a man seeks them consciously or not, for he has introduced a new arbiter into all his enterprises.

The constant practice of these spiritual exercises will inevitably give one the right attitude, the right outlook, and then one need not fear to enter the arena where the world battles are fought, be they the bloodless battles of earning a livelihood or the sanguinary combats of actual war. Only novices, cowards or weaklings need take permanent flight from the struggle of existence to sheltered retreats and monastic life. For with control of mind all things become possible, but without this, man lives to little purpose. *This is inspired activity* and gives a spiritual aim, a lasting meaning, to what would otherwise be a purely ephemeral everyday existence. Such an inspired life represents true sanity. The Western world is really unbalanced, because it is for ever immersed in constant activity without interior compensation. If it would incorporate some kind of spiritual practice into its daily programme, it would not only save itself from the neurasthenic afflictions of the age, not only bring more peace, efficiency and understanding into the management of its affairs, but also achieve a higher life alongside of its working activities.

Thus man may fulfil the unseen and hidden purpose of his being. Then, indeed, as he moves about upon his daily activities, whether in the street and market-place, the home or the factory, *he will be able to say that he is moving about his Father's business*. The secular will have become the sacred.

We may learn the secret of taking the drudgery out of everyday existence by putting the divine into it. All things are symbols of the unseen God. Even work can be a prayer we utter. Every floor that is rightly swept is a pathway for the Lord. No work of ours is so worldly but in it we can show forth the qualities of God. We reveal ourselves by our work. The few who are filled with the spirit of God strive to show forth His perfection in perfectly done work; His wisdom in intelligent work; His power in energetic work. Our highest capacities can be revealed in this way; time can thus be turned to high account, and truths netted in heaven can be brought down to earth.

* * *

A man who depends on others for his help or happiness depends on reeds that may break; but a man who depends on the Overself will never be betrayed.

We may turn to brief considerations of the material help which the Overself renders when we ourselves seem helpless. There is really nothing beyond the scope of such assistance. Ill-health, organic disorders, lack of work, food, shelter, friends or funds, business perplexities, technical problems, distressing relationships—all these and more have been marvellously and divinely adjusted in the experience of various persons known to the writer. They were people who had learnt how to 'tune in' to the Overself, in however small degree, and to throw their burdens on its ampler shoulders. The powerful force of destiny had brought them these sorrows or difficulties, but the all-powerful force of the Overself delivered them in the end.

The economic problem, for example, seems to worry people nowadays as much as any other. Although one who is treading this path may continue to appreciate the value and necessity of money—second greatest power in the world as it is—he will experience less and less that overwhelming thirst for riches which so largely dominates the present age. For as he becomes increasingly aware of the Overself, as the mental steadiness and emotional equilibrium which the practice tends to create percolate increasingly into his everyday attitude, he will feel diminishing anxiety about his material welfare. Indeed, he will believe in the truth of the counsel of Jesus that the Father knows his needs and that he need not make friends with anxiety or despair; but this is not to say that he will degenerate and become apathetic or lazy; he will pay a keener attention to duty and do his work or attend to business more thoroughly and more carefully than ever before, because as already explained he will come to take an almost sacred view of duty.

The secret of all super-personal help is surrender. Not surrender to weakness, lethargy, laziness, hopelessness or shortsighted fatalism, but surrender of the personal power to the central power within oneself. Then, instead of pitting one's own limited faculties against the gloomier circumstances which are arrayed against him in the battles of life, he lets this central power get to work on his behalf. Where one fails, it succeeds; where one perceives only impassable brick walls of difficulty, it passes miraculously through. It will work for him and better than him, yet all that one has to do is to open oneself fully to its expression.

But before one can surrender one must first find the dwelling place of this diviner power. Mere words cannot do it. The path here described takes one right into the centre of that dwelling place. One has to work hard internally to reach this point, but once arrived one is not to labour, only to let oneself be laboured through. One must have the uncommon sense to say: 'I shall interfere no longer. I shall cease this endless calculation of ways and means. I shall put down my load of cares and duties on the ground beside me. I see now what I, in my blindness, refused to see before, that the Overself which supports and carries me, can perform all calculations, manage all affairs, bear all burdens in a manner infinitely better than I could ever do, simply because it is itself infinite in power and wisdom.'

There are times when prudence is but another word for error of judgement; and when a higher kind of prudence is called for, namely, trust in Providence. There are hours when calculation is seen to be but another name for mis-calculation. For the personal mind is limited in outlook, dwarfed in depth beside the immeasurable intuition that arises unerringly from the Overself and, ignoring all distorting masks of men and circumstance, points straight towards the right road. Our cares and anxieties are connected with the personal self, not with the exalted Overself. The elimination of this tyrannous condition depends on the return to the impersonal Overself. Our actions will then no longer be the outcome of mere personal whims, of the ambitions of greed and the desires of possession alone. We shall become clear channels of the Overself, useful instruments in its hands, and impersonal servitors of its divine will. We shall live henceforth without the strain of personal effort, without anxious forethought, knowing that our Father, the Overself, will make all the necessary effort and forethought on our behalf, itself working either through us or through others.

The way is open for all men to conquer the horrors of pain and the heartbreak of poverty, the hardships of failure and the corrosiveness of anxiety, *if only they will conquer their minds*. No problem is too difficult for the Overself to tackle; it would not be the fortifying atom of almighty God within us if it were so feeble as that. No gloomy cloud of pessimism nor peace-destroying nightmare of fear need descend upon any man's life for ever and ever; *the blessed rays of the Overself are with him here and now*, ready to shine benignantly down upon his days as soon as he properly invokes them. The boasted strength of the personal self is really its weakness; true strength lies in that which dwells behind the personal self. We may draw on the infinite, if we will, and thus achieve the seemingly impossible. The powers of the body and the intellect can stretch thus far and no farther, but the powers of the Overself are illimitable.

The divinity which brought our souls into existence, as our mothers brought our bodies into existence, can support, sustain, heal, protect and guide us in precisely the same way that mothers support, sustain, protect and guide their own children. This is not a poetical simile; it is a statement of scientific reality, albeit the reference here is to the science of life. *And no less than every true mother loves her dear child and ever wishes to lead it to real happiness, does the divine Overself love its rebellious offspring, the personal self, and ever seek its true welfare by leading it along the path of repentance and return.* This is the whole message of practical religion, and to instil this truth into our shuttered minds God has sent His prophets among us and will continue to send them so long as we remain errant prodigals and have not the sense to say: 'I will arise and go unto my Father.'

The man who has attained forever the full awareness of the Overself needs neither guidance nor method from anyone else, for a higher power will give him both. But the man who is advancing and has already made some progress in mental quiet can profitably use a simple method of spiritual and material self-help which is always and instantly applicable to every imaginable set of adverse conditions. It will not give everyone everything which he desires, because other forces have something to say in the matter—the forces of destiny, universal evolution and That which created both, God! The personal self must needs fit itself into the cosmic framework which surrounds it, and not expect the framework to be altered to fit it. Nor does it really know what is best for it, what will bring it genuine happiness or true well-being. Suffering is not always to be shirked; sometimes it is a tutor as excellent as any to be found in the best university. We must look on the troubled side of life as spiritual education, and extract the lesson of wisdom from every misfortune. Therefore no method exists, despite the imaginative claims of certain schools, whereby unperfected man can dictate to

God, can *always* avoid misfortune, ill-health, poverty, tragedy, or oppression, and have all his demands satisfied. But a method does exist whereby he may verily make the 'best' of circumstances and relate divine aid, not to his selfish demand but to his true need.

Before the actual exercise is given it will be well to reiterate that only the person who has already developed some degree of mind-strength through the practices of this secret path and mental quiet, can profit by it. We cannot build brick walls without mortar, and we cannot call up spiritual forces without having first prepared some kind of contact with them.

Whoever wishes to invoke the aid of the Overself whenever he is troubled, tried, tempted, hurt, depressed, anxious, worried, undecided or angry—in fact, whenever he is suffering or sinning in any form, should habituate himself to this additional practice. The method is as follows:

One should slow down the rhythm of breathing for two or three minutes and simultaneously question oneself: 'Whom does this trouble?' 'Whom does this pain?' 'Whom does this depress?' 'Whom does this tempt?' or 'Whom does this perplex?'—and so on according to the particular problem. Then a mental pause should be brought about and the thoughts kept calm, concentrated and fixed on the question. Everything else, whether external scenes or extraneous ideas, should be rigidly ignored and the mind introverted until it sinks as deeply into the inner self as the mental quiet practices have been achieved. The entire exercise need not take more than a few minutes and should be done simply and naturally and undemonstratively.

This method is applicable to any kind of problem, which needs only to be brought into the sublime ever-presence of the Overself. Although the latter is quite competent to deal with whatsoever arises, one ought not to make the mistake of always looking for an immediate solution. Higher powers must take their own time, which is normally unpredictable. A striking result may flash forth within the hour or one may have to learn the lesson of quiet patience. These powers have not failed because they refuse to be turned on like a tap.

Impatience breaks their charm and is always detrimental.

When a man has become habituated by long experience to this exercise, he will marvel at its beautiful simplicity and effectiveness, as he relaxes and gently sinks inwards in silent submission of his personal ego. Trying can be very trying.

Whenever discord or disaster of any kind threaten one, this practice may be immediately begun. In this way the mental impression is intercepted and one refuses to identify himself with it. Half the mesmeric harm is thus swept away. The attitude of a vigilant *witness* is adopted, the disturbing impression quickly cut off, and everything undesirable neutralized as one invokes and realizes the Overself. The ordinary man who surrenders to negative thought courts and strengthens the very troubles he wishes to avoid.

Every hurt that threatens, every problem that arises, should be taken at once into the divine centre and contemplated from this newer angle. That is the right way to clarify, heal and enlighten oneself. In the midst of hard difficulties, heart-searing frustrations, crushing defeats or depressing perplexities, a man may yet obtain release by refusing to accept the imposition of conventional thoughts and conventional attitudes. And even when destiny is inexorable and refuses to unbend sufficiently to permit any problem to be solved materially, the latter can always be solved spiritually because it can be eradicated from the mind. Cosmic evolutionary purpose must come into conflict with personal happiness at some time or other, and when it cannot be deflected the practice of spiritual self-recollectedness will unharness the mind of its burden by introducing the radiant light and mystic power of the Overself. But such a method can work effectively only when one possesses the firm faith that the Overself is continuously available and its presence inseparable, when he rejects alertly the thoughts and moods which would drag him like a chained slave from its benign love and mysterious resources, and when he *immediately* displaces worrying, hurtful or degrading sensations by silent unshaken affirmation of his interior existence in the eternal.

Such is the amplitude of this exercise that it can be applied to help others indirectly and to a certain degree. If one has a beloved relative or friend who is in a difficult situation, after having performed the practice, one may picture the person in the mind's eye, and then raise him and his problem aloft to the white light of the Overself in silent blessing. Some illumination or protection will then surely wing its mysterious way through space to that other person.

In every case where a mental problem or material burden has been surrendered rightly to the Overself, a feeling of mental ease and a sense of emotional relief will manifest soon afterwards.

When this habit of swift reference to the Overself by questioning *who* is suffering, *who* is annoyed, and so on, has been fostered until it becomes instinctive, one will feel spiritually secure and materially confident. Although there are determinants of our destiny beyond the span of conscious intention and personal effort, most of us carry unnecessary loads of care. The Overself can bear the same burden far better. Let it — and let us accept its perennial invitation, its gentle guidance, and thus learn to meet life's varied situations with serene equanimity, knowing that its providential care can then never be absent.

Whoever faithfully follows this path will stand still at times with drawn breath when he perceives that a higher will than his own mysteriously intervenes in his affairs and always, in the highest sense, to his ultimate benefit. He will become an effective instrument in its divine hands. All events will become moves on a celestial chessboard. All things will conspire to work out for the best — bitter suffering no less than pleasant joys will provide accepted lessons in fortitude and wisdom. Even the harsh malice of his enemies will not be resented, for he will eventually learn life's last and loftiest secret — that every living creature bears the hidden tokens of divinity within its breast and is unconsciously striving amid its darkest sins for the deathless satisfaction, truth and power which exists in the Overself alone.

4

THE MISSION OF JESUS AND
THE WORK OF THE ADEPT

From *The Inner Reality* (London: Rider & Co., 1939), pp. 249-54, 260-3. (In USA: entitled *Discover Yourself*; 1st edn. rev., York Beach, ME: Samuel Weiser, 1983. Copyright 1983 Kenneth T. Hurst.) Used by permission of Samuel Weiser, Inc., Century Hutchinson Publishing Group, Ltd., and Mr Hurst.

Ignorant men imagine they are self-sufficient. The Adepts are wiser. They know that all they can do is done by God through them. Because they freely permit Him to use them they are perfect instruments and channels for His Truth and Power, while unawakened men are merely instruments and channels for their own personal power.

Because the Adept stands aside and allows the Overself to function through him, he is in that sense equal to God, since he is co-operating with God. All of you who wish to find the Overself, who wish to become Overself-conscious must learn to stand aside in the personal self and become non-obstructive mediums through which it may express.

The spiritual path is simple in essence. Its achievement entails allowing the profound depths of yourself to come to the surface and manifest.

To do this successfully the practice of mental stillness, meditation, is essential. While you are constantly active mentally and physically these depths cannot arise and manifest, but by quieting your mind and your body you provide the right opportunity for the Spirit within to manifest. After training has made you able to do this sufficiently you can again be active without interfering with Its manifestation.

Jesus declares:

I can of mine own self do nothing . . . I seek not mine own will,
but the will of the Father.

The greatest men are the humblest. The smallest are the
most arrogant. Real sages are always modest, claiming no
superiority, and they always put you at your ease. This is
because they have silenced the personal self and become as
children, allowing That which is behind to manifest.

Jesus' hearers could not understand Him. They continued
persecutions. He says to them:

I know you, that ye have not the love of God in you . . . I am
come in my Father's name and ye receive me not: if another shall
come in his own name, him ye will receive.

Jesus represented the Overself, but their grossness could
not recognize this.

These people condemned themselves by their unbelief and
lack of intuition. Only by intuition and never by appearance may you recognize a prophet.

Jesus also reiterates:

I came down from heaven not to do mine own will, but the will
of him that sent me . . . And this is the Father's will which hath
sent me, that everyone which seeth the son and believeth on him
may have everlasting life.

Such then is the Father's will and the reason for Jesus' coming. Those who see and believe in Him may receive the grace
He longs to bestow upon all, but which can only reach those
who accept Him in their hearts with faith and devotion.

For though the Overself sends a Messiah into incarnation
to help mankind, we must co-operate with him in order to
benefit. He asks nothing but the gift of our faith and
devotion.

Jesus knows only His own can come to Him. He says:

All that the Father giveth me shall come to me; and him that
cometh to me I will in no wise cast out.

This is very plain. Those fortunate enough to be incarnated in His time and land can contact him and by inward

recognition answer that claim.

These people had begun the search for the Father and, however dimly, had come into some communion with Him. Jesus knows that their Spiritual Self was drawing them to Him. Others will come and persecute Him, but His son would come and stay.

Then He says:

...He that believeth on me hath everlasting life.

Those believers who accept Him and follow the path He shows can receive His grace. They will eventually come to have that inner awareness of the presence of that eternal Reality which is the everlasting life of Jesus. Then they will know it for their true being.

You will notice that Jesus repeatedly points out that He is an instrument. Even the greatest Messiah is this, a channel, powerless if he has to depend upon his own intellect or mind. Accordingly Jesus asserts:

My doctrine is not mine, but his that sent me.

He tells His listeners, in effect—this truth is not Mine, it is given Me by the Power which illumes Me. You, too, have that Power within you and may become Its instrument. He claims nothing for Himself.

Jesus has to come to look for a few who are His own, knowing that only they are competent to receive His message.

To them He says things which the masses cannot understand, giving them plain, direct truth instead of speaking in the symbols and parables He uses to instruct the multitude.

These few who stand in special relationship to Him are destined to meet the brunt of the persecution dealt out to the first Christians. Because of this they are initiated into the mysteries of the kingdom of heaven. They partake of the strength of its light and receive power which enables them to undergo the persecution.

...But he that entereth in by the door is the shepherd of the sheep ... To him the porter openeth and the sheep heareth his voice; and he calleth his own sheep by name and leadeth them out ...

And when he putteth forth his own sheep he goeth before them and the sheep follow him, for they know his voice.

Jesus knew, before He incarnated, that there were those who through prior evolution had reached the point where the touch of the Master would awaken them to spiritual consciousness.

Those few are to be the bearers of that which He would give mankind. They are incarnated within His lifetime so that He shall find them. They are not merely His followers, but constituted His disciples.

Jesus knows when He goes to preach in the streets that among the multitude there will be four or five who belong to Him. Not to Him personally, but to the power working through Him.

He finds His own! Those destined by their quest for God and Truth in former incarnations to be found of the Master. Those who are ready to receive from Him the reward of illumination. The illumination—He calleth His own sheep by name and leadeth them out.

Jesus goes on to say:

And a stranger they will not follow, but will flee from him: for they know not the voice of strangers.

Trained to know the voice of the shepherd, the sheep will follow no other. Meeting him, his own know they have found the truth for which they seek. Sensing the power which expresses itself through him, they will harken only to his voice.

Predestined from birth to be disciples of their master, any other who attempted to draw them away would be 'a thief and a robber' to whose sheepfold they do not belong. No teacher who has attained truth will seek to take those who do not belong to him. Any so doing have not attained and are but blind leaders of the blind.

Jesus and His disciples reincarnated at the same period as one group. Lost in matter, identified with the body, the disciples spent years finding their way back to the Teacher. But eventually, fulfilling destiny, they came to Him.

Then Jesus said unto them again: verily, verily, I say unto you,

I am the door of the sheep ... All that ever came before me are
thieves and robbers; but the sheep did not hear them.

Here the Master indicates that no other guide, no orthodox
priest or teacher can be the destined leader of 'His own'. All
such are thieves and robbers.

I am the door: by me if any man enter in, he shall be saved and
shall go in and out and find pasture.

Not only for His disciples, but for all his hearers willing
to place complete faith in Him, Jesus is the door; the outlet
through which the Overself can touch their conscious minds.

The Overself is everywhere, but before you can become
aware of it there must be a channel through which it can
connect you. A door by which you may pass to it. That channel must be in the flesh. A human being in whom the Overself is the moving power. No teacher in the invisible world
will do.

So Jesus says:

...if any man enter in, he shall be saved.

What is salvation? Surely it consists of finding that spiritual
truth which will lift you out of ignorance and materiality;
out of the belief that you are only intellect and physical.
Ignorance constitutes the cause of your heavy load of fate,
which you have earned during former lives on this earth.
It hangs over you like a shadow, stored up, waiting for recognition now or in some future birth.

That fate demands expression, readjustment on this earth,
causing you to reincarnate here again and again.

Hence salvation has a double meaning: to free yourself
from your fate and the resulting rebirths into a physical body,
and to be lifted up from the state of spiritual ignorance in
which you exist.

By me if any man enter in he shall be saved.

This means that if you will find your Master and faithfully follow Him and the path He indicates to you, you will
free yourself from your fate and be lifted up out of spiritual
ignorance.

I am come that they might have life and that they might have it more abundantly.

This does not mean physical existence. Jesus came to give you eternal life in the Overself, without beginning or end.

But there is a deeper meaning: I have told you that God is light. That light is the primal substance of this universe. In finding your inner self you find that primal light-current. Until that is done you are only living partially, living in a body and the intellect.

When Jesus states that He came to bring more abundant life, He means that He has come to bring you back to the source of it. The life-current which flows through the universe and through mankind. That which enables your body and mind to function as the heat of the fire in the poker enables it to become red-hot.

★　★　★

People seem to think the Adept is an Adept only if he possesses magical powers, such as healing of the sick or turning water into wine. Jesus performed miracles that He might reach the people.

Miracles, however, are not performed by the power of the Overself, but by that of the mind. Their doing involves the use of a lower faculty and not the faculty of the Divine Self. This the Adept knows, for he expresses truth and truth is a non-mental state.

On the path you begin by finding the outer master. To find the teacher in the flesh is a great achievement. This done he sets you the task of finding Him as the inner teacher. To do that you have to understand that He is not the body which you see, but the soul inside it. At first you see His outer form. Later in your mind's eye you picture His mental image. Then you succeed in realizing Him as a Soul Presence in your heart.

This is a most desirable stage to reach. See the teacher no matter where you are and even if he be thousands of miles away, see him as though he were visibly present.

There is a yet higher stage. Gradually you learn to dismiss the picture and feel only the Presence. Finally the great day comes when your teacher says: 'I have done my work. I withdraw that you may find your own self.'

Then you forget his presence and even him. You find yourself, you are your own light. The teacher's work for you is completed.

Believe me that I am in the Father and the Father in me.

Here is a paradox. Not only is the Divine Overself Atom present within your heart, but you exist within the Overself as the Universal Self.

Spirit all-permeating, filling infinite space, is yet present as a microscopic point within your heart. The Father is in you and you are in the Father.

You have, however, to find the Father's Spirit within you. Until you do you cannot find the Spirit in the Universe.

There are two stages in this search. The first, which you might call mysticism, is the discovery of the Father in you; the discovery of your Soul, the Divine Atom within your heart. This is achieved through meditation, through yoga, aspiration and prayer.

Some time may then elapse. If you keep up the quest God will reward you by bringing you to the Ultimate Path into which your teacher will initiate you.

This is the second stage. This will bring you to the discovery of the Universal, everywhere-present Spirit, and there you complete the cycle. You find the two halves of truth. That which is within and that without you.

To those who have thus attained, Jesus says:

Even the Spirit of Truth; whom the world cannot receive, because it seeth him not, neither knoweth him: but ye know him; for he dwelleth with you and shall be in you.

Intangible, invisible, unfelt, the Infinite Overself is not received by the world because the world cannot see it, and as Jesus says: 'Neither knoweth him.' Nevertheless, though you may be the rankest materialist of this word, yet you cannot get away from the Overself. You are in it and it is in you. Therefore Jesus says: '...but ye know him; for he dwelleth with you.'

In addressing His disciples Jesus tells them:

Peace I leave with you, my peace I give unto you.

That peace is His grace. He gave it only to His disciples because no one else is capable of receiving it. In the disciples this gift of grace manifests as it always does at first by burning aspiration for spiritual realization. When the teacher fans the spark of spiritual yearning in the seeker's heart the latter begins to search more desperately than ever before.

His aspiration intensely speeded up by the teacher's bestowal of grace, the seeker may pass through a period of unhappiness, turmoil, and unsatisfied spiritual longing.

This thirsting and burning for spiritual realization is the result of the contact made in the heart with the teacher. It may be so poignant that fits of weeping may come and continue for long periods.

Through it all the seeker knows a strange inner peace. The more he experiences the weeping periods the more grace is being bestowed upon him. The tears are the expression of an unconscious recognition of the distance between the present stage and that ultimate one which is sought and which is the true home. Though it may last several weeks, or months, or even years, varying with individuals, this stage will pass.

With the coming of the second stage the turmoil dies down, and the Master's peace appears increasingly in the heart. Therefore, Jesus says: '...my peace I give unto you.'

This very peace, however, may begin as the most heart-rending spiritual agony.

Abide in me, and I in you...I am the vine and ye are the branches. If my words abide in you, ye shall ask what ye will and it shall be done unto you.

These words of Jesus mean that from the moment you find your destined teacher you must hand over your inner life completely. Not to him, but to the higher power working through him. In him you have a bridge whereby you may reach the Overself. You must use it, trusting always to that higher power and intelligence.

You have only to think of your teacher to achieve realization of power. Jesus defined it thus '...my words abide in you...' This means that His truth abides in you.

5

THE BIRTH OF THE UNIVERSE

From *The Wisdom of the Overself* (London: Rider & Co., 1943), pp. 44-56. (In USA: 2nd edn. rev., York Beach, ME: Samuel Weiser, 1984. Copyright Kenneth T. Hurst.) Used by permission of the publisher and Mr Hurst.

Certain thoughts will come naturally to the student's mind at this stage. If we take an historic view of the universe we are confronted by three connected questions which have framed themselves on the lips and troubled themselves into the heads of every cultured race of antiquity, of the medieval period and of modern times. They are: When did the world begin? Whence did it come? How did it arise?

The cosmology of the hidden teaching begins its answer to these questions by explaining that the universe is an endless affair. There is no moment at which it has not existed, either latently or actively, and consequently there will be no moment when it will not continue to exist, either latently or actively. This is so because the world does not arise by a sudden act of creation but by a gradual process of manifestation. For being a vast thought and not a vast thing, it is brought into being by the World-Mind out of *itself*, out of its own mental 'substance', and not out of any extraneous stuff such as matter is supposed to be by materialists — whether they be scientific, religious or metaphysical materialists. The World-Mind does not have to put out metaphorical hands at some specific moment and begin to mould matter, like a potter moulding his clay into the shape of a cosmos.

The cosmos, being a thought-formation, can never really disappear any more than a human idea can really disappear when it is put aside from attention. We may understand this point better by considering how thoughts exist in a man's mind. What happens to them when they vanish? Where do they come from when they appear? At any time he can call them up again even though during the interval they have seemingly been non-existent. His ideas are manifestations of his own mind, not creations out of some external stuff. In the same way the World-Mind manifests something of its own self in the cosmos. And its own self, as will be shown later, being uniquely eternal and undying, it is inevitable that the world-ideas which have arisen within it are eternal and undying, too.

Thus there is no particular moment in the universe's long history when it could be said to have been first created. It has never had a beginning and consequently will never have an end. It has never been started so it can never be finished. It is eternal because the stuff to which we can ultimately trace it is nothing else than Mind, to which there is no conceivable beginning and no conceivable end. Mind is what it has been since the beginningless incalculable past; as Buddha said: 'unborn, uncreate, unoriginated.' There is no first or last moment for it.

This tenet is usually illustrated in the hidden teaching by asking the student to draw a circle. The point whence he commenced to draw it marks its beginning and the point where he stopped marks its end. He must think of this circle as a *type*, standing for all the circles which ever existed. It will then be impossible for him to assign any particular point as its actual beginning or end. The points previously marked were merely temporary. The circle is then understood to be really an endless and beginningless figure. Even if it be said that the universe was specially created on a particular historic day, as the founders of religions are compelled to say when they address the masses who, being ignorant of the true mentalistic character of time, take it to be something absolute and fixed, this day can be but a temporary mark at best. It is like the temporary mark on the student's circle, for there is no moment when Mind was not. The manifestations of Mind have therefore always been in either abstract or concrete existence. The Swastika-wheel of the universe gyrates without end.

It is a scientifically-ascertained fact that the planets and stars and nebulae which light up the firmament are of different ages. Some are young and others are old; some are almost new-born but others are dying. Therefore the belief that once upon a time God suddenly created the world—which would make all these astronomical bodies of equal age today—is not an acceptable one. It is more reasonable to believe, with the hidden teaching, that the universe never had a beginning and will never have an ending, that it is eternal and self-sustaining because it is the body of God—if we like to use this much-misused term—who is eternal and self-sustaining, and that a perpetual evolution of the entire universe and its creatures is constantly proceeding.

Whoever can perceive this will then be able to perceive its corollary: that causality is only a temporary truth, a mere mark like the one which is used tentatively to begin the tracing out of a circle, and that ultimately there is no real first cause and no real final effect anywhere in this series of things without a stop. Nothing exists by itself and all things exist today as an indirect consequence of innumerable causes stretching like an endless chain through the beginningless past. Whoever can comprehend that every event is somehow connected with innumerable other events, that a web of inter-dependence is thrown across all things without exception, can also comprehend that no single manifested thing can be self-sufficient, or self-existent in the full meaning of the term nor even as having a single cause or a single effect.

We naturally forget that what we ordinarily consider to be the obvious cause of an event is only an outstanding and final moment in a host of untraceable earlier changes which converged and met in it. We also overlook that what we ordinarily consider the creation of a new thing is only the latest fruit of the indirect co-operation of innumerable older things. Under such conditions of an infinite regress of causes which are only pseudo-causes and effects which are only pseudo-effects, the question when the world was created is not a proper one because the problem has intially been misstated. There are certain erroneous presuppositions implied in these interrogative words. Such a question cannot therefore be answered, not because philosophy is ignorant, but because the question itself is not rightly put.

The universe is therefore as old or as eternal as the World-Mind itself. It is an idea, but nevertheless it is an everlasting idea. Creation begins and ends nowhere and nowhen. There is no place or moment of which the first cause or final effect can be stated with certitude. How then can the starting-point of the entire creative process be defined? How then can we make any selection which shall be other than arbitrary at all from this endless series of inter-connected events? Whichever one is chosen will be the beginning of creation only from a most superficial view. How nebulous is the conception of the universe which presumes to assign a 'date' to creation! Every such date will vary with the mere caprice of the 'dater'; he will hatch out a creation theory to suit himself. It will depend on human temperament or taste.

The world is a complex of countless numbers of connected events. Consequently no absolute single cause can be strictly assigned to any single event. From the fact that however far we attempt to trace back to a first cause of the universe, we find every so-called cause itself to have its origin in a preceding cause, and that the latter is in its turn the effect produced by a previous cause, it is right and reasonable to infer that there is no beginning in the universe and consequently there can be no end. This means that the process of ever-becoming is an eternal one and is the very law of the universe's own being. For no particular thing is a cause alone or an effect alone but must always be both at the same time.

Such a situation demolishes the metaphysical truth of the old notion of causality, although it leaves it quite untouched for practical purposes. It cancels the *ultimate* truth of the law of cause and effect which governs all world phenomena, although it leaves its *immediate* truth untouched. When we recognize that the chain of reciprocally-dependent links which constitutes a cause is beginningless and endless we have to drop causality as a metaphysical principle. This must not be misunderstood. We are not here speaking from the practical and scientific standpoint but from the philosophic one. We are saying only that an *adequate* cause cannot be found by finite human intelligence but only some of the factors contributing to such a cause. Beyond this it is impossible to go. There will always be other factors which have not been ascertained. In theological words, God alone knows all.

If, philosophically, the notion of a sudden first creation is an untenable assumption, the related notion of the possibility of creating something out of nothing is equally untenable. But the believers in a Deity made in man's magnified image ascribe the genesis of the universe to just such an act.

Looked at from the outside, the universe comes forth out of nothingness and passes away into nothingness. But looked at from inside, there has always been an eternal hidden reality in its back-ground. This reality is Mind. The world is only its manifestation. For if every effect is previously contained in its cause and that again is confined in what preceded it, the chain goes back and back and stops only when it stops with the source of all ideas—Mind. Thus Mind embraces all things but is itself embraced by none. Hence Mentalism teaches that the universe has the same origin as any idea, that is, in and for a mind; therefore the correct way to regard the relation between the universe and its originator is to see it as being similar to the relation between any human idea and the mind in which it is begotten. The World-Mind does not need to 'create' the universe out of nothing when it can bring it to birth out of its own self. And as a mental principle it does this by projecting the world as its idea. The world is its self-projection.

How did the universe come to assume the character which it possesses? This is answered by the doctrine of mentalism. Mind or rather World-Mind is immanent throughout the universe. The universe has arisen out of its constructive meditation but it has arisen in orderly self-determined fashion shaped by its own memorized mental impressions of a former state of active existence. The ceaseless procession of images, picturing forth suns and stars, lands and seas and all things visible emanate from the World-Mind, under a divine immutable mysterious karmic law like water trickling from an inexhaustible fountain.

Karma is a twofold law, one being general and the other special. The first is ultimate, and applicable to everything in the universe for it is simply the law of every individual entity's own continuity. Whether it be a planet or a protoplasm it has to inherit the characteristics of its own previous existence and thus adjust effect to cause. The second is immediate, and applicable only to individuals who have attained self-consciousness, thus limiting the start of its operations to human entities. This makes the individual accountable for thoughts and for the deeds born of his thoughts.

It is through mutually-acting karmic processes that this universe becomes possible. The World-Mind brings forth its general world-images not by any arbitrary fiat but by their natural continuity as the consequences of all those that have previously existed. They are a continuation of all the remembered world-images which have appeared before, but modified and developed by their own mutual inter-action and evolution, not by the capricious decree of a humanized God. The World-Mind makes the universe by constructively thinking it. But it does not think arbitrarily. The thoughts arise of their own accord under a strict karmic and evolutionary law. It must be emphasized that on this view the universe constitutes a self-actuating system, although it must equally be understood that the system itself depends on World-Mind for its own continued existence and continuous activity. All the karmic forces and thought-forms carry on their mutual activities, intertwine, interact and evolve of their own accord in the presence of the World-Mind just as plants grow of their own accord in the presence of sunlight. But it is to that very presence that they owe their own sustenance and existence.

All this pre-supposes a prior existence of the universe wherein its present general karma was made. We have already seen that the cosmos itself is continuous, and that its past is beginningless. But intervals of non-existence periodically interrupt its history. These are only temporary, however.

There are no real breaks in its existence but there are apparent ones when it lapses into latency. For it rotates through changing phases. Each successive appearance of the remanifested universe follows inevitably after the one which has previously gone into a latent state. When the collective karmas of all individual and planetary centres exhaust themselves, a cycle of world history closes. The manifested universe then retreats and the World-Mind rests from its labours. But dawn follows night and the cosmic dawn witnesses the re-imagining of all things once again. When the same karmas begin once more to germinate and to reproduce themselves a new cycle opens and the visible world comes into being once more as the heritage of all the existences which were to be found in the previous one. The characteristics of a previous cosmos determine the nature of the one which succeeds it.

This antithesis of work and rest, of Becoming and Being, of a rhythm curiously like that of the in-breathing and out-breathing of living creatures, immediately confronts us when we try to understand the World-Mind's relation to the universe. The present universe is not the first which has manifested nor will it be the last. Each separate world-system —such as the present one—is merely a unit in a beginningless and endless series. In this sense only is the universe indestructible. Each is a heritage from the one that existed before, a precipitation of karmas which have succeeded in bringing about their own realization.

The history of universal existence is therefore the history of an endless chain of alternations between potential being and actual becoming. Thus the universe is undergoing an evolution which is being worked out according to strict karmic law and not by mere chance, as materialists think, nor by arbitrary commands of a personal creator, as religionists think. The modern scientific notion of evolution is only a half-truth. The real process is a rhythm of growth and decay, evolution and dissolution, following each other with inevitable sequence. It is the combination of these two phases which makes up a universal movement that knows no finality. If cosmic nebulae develop into solar systems, these in turn dissolve eventually into cosmic nebulae again. The universe of forms ever returns to its starting point: it is without beginning and will be without end; this is why it is subject to birth and death, degeneration and renewal, that is to *change*. It is like an ever-rolling wheel moving onward through these alternating aeons of activity and rest. Hence the ancient teachers represented it under the figure of a revolving Swastika-wheel.

THE KARMIC IMPRESSIONS

The mysterious working of karma, this force which moulds the conditions of every centre of being from protoplasmic cell to vast cosmos, must next be uncovered. If the world were nothing but a collection of material objects karma could never come into play. But because it is, as mentalism shows, a collection of thought-formations and because there is a World-Mind as the unitary ground connecting all these formations, the possibility of karma as an operative force exists. For karma would be meaningless if there were not some kind of orderly continuity between the past, the present and the future of all those things and creatures which make up the universal existence. But this implies that Nature must keep and conserve some sort of memory in her secret recesses.

If every individual preserves a record of his own history, why should it seem fantastic for the World-Mind to preserve a record of its own history? And because its existence is inseparable from the manifested cosmos, in doing this it preserves an all-comprehensive record of the universe's own history, too. No thought, no event, no object, no scene and no figure has ever been wholly lost. This implies that the memories of globes and stars and nebulae utterly remote in space and time are still preserved. But human imagination must stagger away from the boundless consequences of this truth, its finite limitations here defeating its own activity. And because memory is not an object which the sense can grasp but something entirely immaterial, this in turn involves the existence of something mental. A mental principle which shall be cosmic in its spatial sweep and permanent in its embrace of time, is and can be none other than the World-Mind itself. Thus the foundation of all karmic working can be traced to the World-Mind. The rise, abiding and dissolution of karma is indeed a twin-function to that of its ideation.

We have learnt that in the end everything must return to its divine source, if not before by its own evolution then certainly at the end of a cosmic cycle by the universal rhythmic dissolving movement which then attains its climax. If we turn backward in thought to such a time when the universe was not in visible tangible existence, to one of those cosmic periods when the World-Mind had taken in its breath as it were, we find a mysterious state of nothingness that is yet not a nothingness. Mind alone is, a great Void alone reigns, it is as if there were no existence at all. There is not a thing, not a thought and not a creature. Nevertheless the *possibilities* of the birth of all things, all thoughts and creatures do somehow exist. Just as different sound-forms are latently stored in the tracks which have been made on the surface of a gramophone record, so different thought-forms are latently stored by karma during a period of universal rest within the World-Mind. And everything in the universe without exception being such a form or collection of forms, it follows that everything will then still have a potential existence. Just as a massive oak tree once had an invisible and intangible existence in the acorn or the gentle fragrance of a white flower once had an unsmelt existence in the tiny seed, so the earth and stars and sun which we see around us today once had an immaterial existence in the germinal form which their own karma had stored within the memory of the World-Mind. Every starry body in the firmament with its particular distinguishing characteristics and every creature which dwelt upon it with its own desires, tendencies and capacities were memorized by the wonderful faculties of World-Mind. From this it will be seen that memory played a potent part in creating the world of which we are conscious. During these periods of its own suppression, therefore, the universe still existed as a seed-like possibility.

The World-Mind is all-containing. Since the beginningless past it has gathered these cosmic memories. The patterns of all that goes to constitute a universe previously existed in it in this potential form. The archetype of everything found in Nature first existed in this illimitable storehouse. Just as the silent registrations on a gramophone record are converted under suitable conditions into vividly heard words so the invisible registrations in World-Mind were converted at the ripe karmic time into vividly-experienced things. Just as shouts uttered in a narrow mountain ravine call forth echoing sounds, so the karmic impressions stored during a cosmic night, repeated themselves in the space-time world as they passed into actuality and thus appeared again in tangible visible form.

We must not make the materialist mistake of regarding this universal mind as though it were a kind of box in which the myriad thought-forms which totalize into a universe, are piled up. The thoughts originally pre-exist in it not concretely but in the abstract sense that ideas of an intended effect pre-exist in a musician's mind. Such pre-existence of the world-ideas is possible only through the agency of karma. If our finite human mind can latently hold so many and so different ideas at one and the same time, why should not the infinite World-Mind find it possible to hold the innumerable units which sum up as the whole world-idea?

This karmic seed-form must not be misunderstood. Because everything is really mental, because everything is a thought-formation, the memorization of it held by the World-Mind is not a second and separate substance but is the very essence or soul of the thing itself. If we compare the World-Mind to a piece of wax then the impression made on the latter by a mental seal represents the memorized unmanifested world and the force or pressure applied to the seal represents karma. And just as the moulded picture is not distinct from the wax itself so the innumerable karmic impressions which compose the memory-image of the whole universe, which is but a great thought, are not distinct from the World-Mind too.

A man forgets his own life and the external world during deep sleep but remembers them completely again the following morning. If all his ideas are latently and mysteriously preserved during the sleep state despite apparent annihilation, then we have a hint from Nature to help us understand how it is possible for all the ideas of the World-Mind to be latently and mysteriously preserved even when they are no longer actualized during the cosmic night. Just as not a single thought-form is really lost by the individual mind during sleep so not a single thought-form is lost by the World-Mind when a cosmic period closes and everything vanishes into apparent nothingness, but really returns to the original unity whence it earlier proceeded.

The karmic impressions are so subtle and so abstract from the human standpoint that a further analogy may help to clarify their meaning. A poet, by which we do not mean a mere versifier, who sits down to write an imaginative poem will not in the beginning know the precise sentences and exact words which his poem will contain nor the full course and final shape which it will take. He will most likely feel some vague intuitions and uncalculated inspirations pressing within him for expression and only as he goes on to create definite word-forms for them does he begin to see his way more clearly. What is happening? The actual and spontaneous composition and progressive development of the poem has brought down into this space-time world of visible forms something which previously had existed in his so-called unconscious mind only as a mental possibility. In the same way the universe in its potential state is a mental possibility existing in the World-Mind, a possibility which has no graspable existence until it appears in actuality as a visible form. Every thought-formation—which means every thing —that exists in this world is born of its corresponding impression in the formless world. The volume and variety of world-appearances arise from the impressions which have resided since the beginningless past in an unbroken chain of continuous transformations in the World-Mind. Every activity, every existence leaves its impress in the World-Mind and the cumulative result of all these combined impressions displays itself eventually as the universe.

Thus the general karmic memories of the unmanifested world, like invisible pictures upon a sensitive photographic film which wait for the time when they shall be developed into visibility, rest in the World-Mind and wait for the time when they become activated. Then their energies are released and cause the springing to life of a fresh cosmic manifestation. When the necessary cyclic hour strikes, the potential planetary and cosmic thought-forms amassed within the World-Mind since the incalculable past become self-active, just as when the necessary wind or lunar influence is ready the ocean manifests its potential waves. The sum-total of all the impressions which thus become actualized, the heritage of all the forms and lives constitutes a cosmos.

To make the next point clear let us return to our early and elementary study of the way we receive knowledge of external things. The vibration which travels from the surface-sense along a nerve path to cells in the brain-cortex, is concerned only with separate sensations. When these are associated, co-ordinated and brought into consciousness as seeing, hearing and so on, the sense-experience becomes a percept. When such a percept is stored in the mind and later recalled or reproduced, then the faculty of memory comes into play. A little reflection will show that this faculty is merely a particular form taken by the image-making power of the mind. If the human mind memorizes through the use of its imagination, then the World-Mind must in its larger way use the same faculty too. If this point is understood then it will be easier to grasp the next point, that karma, being the kinetic memory of Nature, is necessarily coupled with the imaginative power of Nature.

It is thus out of these stored memories, that is imaginations of innumerable forms, that the World-Mind recalls, constructs and evolves everything. The seed-memories of the world-idea, retained and transmitted since an earlier cycle, revive, re-appear and develop through the mysterious memorizing and imaginative powers of World-Mind. But it does not activate them in a chaotic or an arbitrary manner. On the contrary there is orderly sequence in the process, for each of the myriad thought-forms contained in the world-idea is at every stage of its history an inheritance from that which preceded it.

All the potential thought-forms are not brought into activity simultaneously. Out of the innumerable host available, a selective process inherent in the intelligence of the World-Mind and working always with the immutable law of karma, accepts, associates and gathers together those only which make for a gradual unfoldment in time and an orderly unfoldment in space. They do not emerge altogether but successively. Hence the universe never appears as ready-made, but as a gradual evolution.

Through its power of constructive imagination, *which is its first characteristic*, the World-Mind brings the cosmos into being. It can emanate anything because imagination, the most plastic of all elements, is its central activity. There is no limit to the metamorphoses of forms which imagination can take. Consequently, there is no limit to the evolution of forms which we behold around us in the universe. The fecundity of images which the World-Mind has put forth is thus easily explicable. If it is possible for the finite imagination of man to produce a wonderful variety of forms and patterns in his arts and crafts why should it not be still more possible for the infinite imagination of World-Mind to produce, under karma of course, the innumerable host of forms and patterns which crowd the universe? Hence there are countless other solar systems in the cosmos besides our own, containing every type of living creature in a diversity far beyond the most fantastic imagination of man.

The history of the progressive unfoldment of the universal picture is thus but a history of the protean transformations of the multiplied images which subsist in the World-Mind. Creation on this view, is simply Mind's protean power to assume any and every form which it chooses; it is essentially a process of imagination. But in the end it does not matter whether we say that World-Mind is imagining or willing or thinking or constructing or dreaming the universe for all these activities must necessarily be one and the same to it. We may better understand this point by asking ourself: Is there any psychological difference between the states of the novelist so absorbed in the highest pitch of creativeness as to be carried away by the adventures of his hero, the religious mystic rapt in perfect contemplation of the sufferings on the Cross to the point of producing stigmata, and the dreamer so caught in an intensely vivid nightmare as to awaken trembling with fear? All these states necessarily include and synthesize will, thought, imagination, creativeness and dreaming.

Under an infinite diversity of forms World-Mind is forever manifesting itself. Just as under the very multitudinousness of a dreamer's dream-creation there lies buried the fact of the singleness and unity of the dreaming mind, so under the very multitudinousness of things in the waking realm there lies buried the fact that they are all manifestations of one and the same Mind. And just as the separateness of the dreamer's world exists only on the surface and is secretly connected with him, so the separateness of the waking world exists only as a surface impression. In the end there is really a unity.

PART TWO

READINGS FROM THE POSTHUMOUSLY PUBLISHED NOTEBOOKS

Note: References to paragraphs from the Notebooks are given by volume number (in Roman numerals), category number, and page number within the category. See Bibliography for a list of the 16 volumes and 28 categories.

1

THE QUEST

XV.24.85-6

Each personal existence has its place to fill here in life and its development to undergo, but it is given a higher meaning than the animal's only as it is sought and found. Neither psychology nor physiology, neither metaphysics, religion, nor mysticism can each by itself sufficiently explain the human being. If, however, they work together in harmony they come much nearer to this goal; but their totality is still incomplete. The last turn of the key is philosophy. Thereafter the final revelation must come by itself, by grace, for man has then removed the obstruction, the tyranny of his own little self. If the ego remains to live and act in the world, whether busy in doing or lost in meditation, it is a purified, a surrendered being. But it has not surrendered to other egos. Even the gurus, however reputed and respected, can teach and lead others only by the path along which they themselves came. Their work can be helpful, valuable, encouraging; but at a certain point, when apprenticeship must give way to proficiency, it can become repetitive and restrictive. After that, the courage and strength to obey the Voice of the Silence, sought and given by the Silence itself, must alone lead him.

XIII.19.27-8

We hear from the East that the world is unreal and that the ego is unreal, or that the world does not exist and that the ego does not exist. It is here that semantics as developed by

Western minds may perhaps be of some service in clarify-
ing confused thinking leading to confused statements. The
body is a part of the world. Do we or do we not dwell in
a body? If we do not then we should stop feeding it and stop
taking it to the physician when it gets sick. Yet even those
people who make such extraordinary statements do continue
to eat, to fall sick, and to visit a doctor. Surely that disposes
immediately of the question whether or not the body exists.
In the same way and by the same pattern of reasoning we
can discover that the world also exists. What then has led
these Indian teachers to proclaim otherwise? Here we begin
to intrude upon the field of mentalism and as a necessary
part of the key to mentalism we must return to the dream
state. If we dream of a world around us and of a body in
which we live in this dream world and of other bodies of
other persons moving in it, the Indians say that these dream
persons and this dream world are seen to be non-existent
when we wake up and hence they deny its reality. But the
experience did happen, so let us scrutinize it. There was no
such thing as this world, true, but something was there; what
was there? Thoughts. All this world and all these persons
about whom we dream pass through consciousness as
thoughts, so the thoughts were there. Whether we consider
dream or hallucination, the pictures are there in the person's
mind; they exist there, but they exist there only as mental
creations. But when we say they are merely mental creations, we are bringing in an attempt to judge them, to judge
their nature, what they really are. The statement that they
are unreal is therefore a judgement and is acceptable only
on the basis of a particular standpoint, the standpoint of the
observer who is outside the dream, outside the hallucination. It is not acceptable on the basis of the person who is
having the experience at that moment. Thus we see that the
existence of the ego, the body, and the world need not be
denied; it is there, it is part of our experience, but what we
have to do is examine it more closely and attempt a judgement of its nature. And this judgement does not alter the
fact that they are being experienced. This is a fact of our
own, of everyone's experience, including the highest sage,

only the sage and the common man each has his own judgement from his point of view, from his knowledge. In all these
topics we can see how much easier it is to pick our way if
we adopt the attitude which was proclaimed in *The Hidden
Teaching Beyond Yoga* that there is a double viewpoint and a
double standard in this teaching in order that we may be
clear about our experiences and about our ideas and not get
them mixed up. These two standpoints, the immediate and
the ultimate, the common and the philosophic, are absolutely
necessary in all talk and study about such metaphysical
topics. Otherwise we get lost in mere verbiage, words, words,
words.

XIII.19.16

If we think, 'I strive to become one with God,' or, 'I am one
with God,' we have unconsciously denied the statement itself
because we have unconsciously set up and retained two
things, the 'I' and 'God'. If these two ultimately exist as
separate things they will always exist as such. If, however,
they really enter into union, then they must always have been
in union and never apart. In that case, the quest of the underself for the Overself is unnecessary. How can these two
opposed situations be resolved? The answer is that relativity has taught us the need of a double standpoint, the one
relative and practical and constantly shifting, the other absolute and philosophical and forever unchanged. From the first
standpoint we see the necessity and must obey the urge of
undertaking this quest in all its practical details and successive stages. From the second one, however, we see that all
existence, inclusive of our own and whether we are aware
of it or not, dwells in a timeless, motionless Now, a changeless, actionless Here, a thingless, egoless Void. The first bids
us work and work hard at self-development in meditation,
metaphysics, and altruistic activity, but the second informs
us that nothing we do or abstain from doing can raise us
to a region where we already are and forever shall be in any
case. And because we are what we are, because we are
Sphinxes with angelic heads and animal bodies, we are forced
to hold *both* these standpoints side by side. If we wish to think

truthfully and not merely half-truthfully, we must make both these extremes meet one another. That is, neither may be asserted alone and neither may be denied alone. It is easier to experience this quality than to understand it.

This is puzzling indeed and can never be easy, but then, were life less simple and less paradoxical than it is, all its major problems would not have worried the wisest men from the remotest antiquity until today. Such is the paradox of life and we had better accept it. That is, we must not hold one standpoint to the detriment of the other. These two views need not oppose themselves against each other but can exist in a state of reconciliation and harmony when their mutal necessity is understood. We have to remember both that which is ever-becoming and that which is ever in being. We are already as eternal, as immortal, as divine as we ever shall be. But if we want to become aware of it, why then we must climb down to the lower standpoint and pursue the quest in travail and limitation.

XIII.20.217

Two things have to be learned in this quest. The first is the art of mind-stilling, of emptying consciousness of every thought and form whatsoever. This is mysticism or Yoga. The disciple's ascent should not stop at the contemplation of anything that has shape or history, name or habitation, however powerfully helpful this may have formerly been to the ascent itself. Only in the mysterious void of Pure Spirit, in the undifferentiated Mind, lies his last goal as a mystic. The second is to grasp the essential nature of the ego and of the universe and to obtain direct perception that both are nothing but a series of ideas which unfold themselves within our minds. This is the metaphysics of Truth. The combination of these two activities brings about the realization of his true Being as the ever beautiful and eternally beneficent Overself. This is philosophy.

XIII.21.75

We, the universe, everything, are pure Mind. This is un-

changeable, hence unevolutable, or it could not be the Real.
Once you awaken to IT you know it always was what it is;
it can never evolve. All the rest was a kind of self-hypnoti-
zation, hence unreal. In that sense the Garden of Eden story
is correct. We were then immortal, immaterial, innocent. We
lost this by losing our awareness and accepting a limited idea
of ourselves. We have been driven out of the Garden because
we wanted knowledge. Knowledge presupposes 'a second
thing' — something to be known. Thus we lost unity, sought
a world of objects, and got into oblivion of self. The happy
Edenic state can be restored by right thinking and de-
hypnotization of ourselves.

XVI.26.96

Man, in his earlier phases of being, was connected with the
Overself and aware of it. But his connection lacked his own
control. Eventually, to fulfil the purpose of evolution, he lost
this connection and with it his awareness. Now he has to
regain the connection and reawaken this awareness by his
own efforts and out of his own inner activity, through his
own desiring and in his own individual freedom. What has
he gained by this change to compensate the loss? His consciousness has become more sharply focused and consequently more clearly aware.

XIII.19.4

Only when one stands upon this mystical mountain top does
one begin to see how, in a made universe, there cannot be
the pleasurable, the joyful, and the sweet alone. Wherever
there is birth there must be death; wherever there is a possible pleasure there must be a possible pain. The recognition of the unpleasant things may sound quite inhuman, and
in a certain sense it is; but then, it was not a human being
who fashioned the universe.

VI.9.163

The sun, planets, and stars must move in their regular orbits.
They are not free to change their course each day. Can this

little creature, man—a mere speck on one of them—claim a larger freedom than theirs without being insane?

VI.9.102–3

Atlantis shaped itself out of the condensing fire mists. Land hardened. Animals appeared. Men and women appeared. Civilizations appeared. The continent was developed. Then the wheel turned. The continent sank and all went with it. In 1919, Germany lay at the feet of her victors. She was disarmed and dismembered. She was weak, depressed, and fearful. Nobody was afraid of her. The wheels turned. Germany armed to the teeth. Her frontiers grew. She was strong, optimistic, and aggressive. Everybody was afraid of her. Today she is again disarmed, weak and fearful. Arabia was unknown, insignificant, unimportant, obscure, her people barbarous, semi-savage. The wheel turned. A prophet arose, instructed and inspired his people. They spread out and took an empire that spread from the Atlantic to China. The wheel turned. The Arab power dwindled again. Arabia itself became a mere province, or colony, of the Turks. Empires are formed but to dissolve again; continents rise but to sink. Peoples collect but to be redistributed once more. Cycles operate, the wheel turns, evolution becomes involution. Only the intellectually blind, the spiritually paralysed can fail to perceive this. And the seeker of truth needs to be brave to be a hero, if he would tear down the veil and behold the Goddess Isis as she really is. Our own decade [1940s] has witnessed strange things but things which prove this truth up to the hilt.

XV.24.9–10

All previous experience should teach him that it is not safe to be too happy, that he cannot live on the heights of joy for too long with impunity. It is not safe to exult too freely in the good fortune which comes in the summers of life; it is not safe to forget the hours of bad fortune which came in the winters of life. Fate cannot be trusted to bring in only such pleasant hours, for it may equalize itself by hurting him now and then. He should temper his delight at fate with fear of it. But even this is not an ideal attitude. Serenity, which leaves him above both delight and fear, is immensely better.

XV.24.14

If suffering brings moods of dejection, it is only fulfilling its intention. This is part of its place in the scheme of things, leading to the awareness that underneath the sweet pleasures of life there is always pain. But thought would present only a half-truth if it stopped there. The other half is much harder to find: it is that underneath the surface sufferings which no one escapes, far deeper down than its counterpart, is a vast harmony, an immense love, an incredible peace, and a universal support.

XV.24.14

Joy and sorrow are, after all, only states of mind. He who gets his mind under control, keeping it unshakably serene, will not let these usurpers gain entry. They do not come from the best part of himself. They come from the ego. How many persons could learn from him to give up their unhappiness if they learnt that most of their sorrows are mental states, the false ego pitying itself?

XIII.19.28

The difficulty in accommodating the practical and philosophical views of existence is understandable. However, these dual views should not be mistaken for contrasting and opposing ones. The ultimate insight synthesizes them although it cannot prevent the continuance of their seeming variations. It is as though the foreground of the mind must hold the practical view while the background simultaneously holds a philosophical view. This is true for the developed aspirant, but in the adept there arrives, after long practice and profound experience, a condition of illumination which treats all experience for the idea that it is and at the same time keeps bright the light of the ever-burning lamp of reality—Pure Mind.

XIII.19.24

He has to practise living on two different planes of being at once, the immediate and ultimate, the short-range and long-range, the relative and the Absolute, not as if they were in eternal contradiction but as if they were one and indivisible.

XIII.20.26-7

The quest has three aspects: metaphysical, meditational, and morally active. It is the metaphysician's business to think this thing called life through to its farthest end. It is the mystic's business to intuit the peaceful desireless state of thoughtlessness. But this quest cannot be conducted in compartments; rather must it be conducted as we have to live, that is, integrally. Hence it is the philosopher's business to bring the metaphysician's bloodless conclusions and the mystic's serene intuition into intimate relation with practical human obligations and flesh-and-blood activities. Both ancient mystical-metaphysical wisdom and modern scientific practicality form the two halves of a complete and comprehensive human culture. Both are required by a man who wants to be fully educated; one without the help of the other will be lame. This may well be why wise Emerson confessed, 'I have not yet seen a man!' Consequently, he who has passed through all the different disciplines will be a valuable member of society. For meditation will have calmed his temperament and disciplined his character; the metaphysics of truth will have sharpened his intelligence, protected him against error, and balanced his outlook; the philosophic ethos will have purified his motives and promoted his altruism, while the philosophic insight will have made him forever aware that he is an inhabitant of the country of the Overself. He will have touched life at its principal points yet will have permitted himself to be cramped and confined by none.

XIII.20.27-8

He who has sufficiently purified his character, controlled his senses, developed his reason, and unfolded his intuition is always ready to meet what comes and to meet it aright. He need not fear the future. Time is on his side. For he has stopped adding bad karma to his account and every fresh year adds good karma instead. And even where he must still bear the workings of the old adverse karma, he will still remain serene because he understands with Epictetus that: 'There is only one thing for which God has sent me into the world, and that is to perfect my nature in all sorts of virtue or strength; and there is nothing that I cannot use for that purpose.' He knows that each experience which comes to him is what he most needs at the time, even though it be what he likes least. He needs it because it is in part nothing else than his own past thinking, feeling, and doing come back to confront him to enable him to see and study their results in a plain, concrete, unmistakable form. He makes use of every situation to help his ultimate aims, even though it may hinder his immediate ones. Such serenity in the face of adversity must not be mistaken for supine fatalism or a lethargic acceptance of every untoward event as God's will. For although he will seek to understand why it has happened to him and master the lesson behind it, he will also seek to master the event itself and not be content to endure it helplessly. Thus, when all happenings become serviceable to him and when he knows that his own reaction to them will be dictated by wisdom and virtue, the future can no more frighten him than the present can intimidate him. He cannot go amiss whatever happens. For he knows too, whether it be a defeat or a sorrow in the world's eyes, whether it be a triumph or joy, the experience will leave him better, wiser, and stronger than it found him, more prepared for the next one to come. The philosophic student knows that he is here to face, understand, and master precisely those events, conditions, and situations which others wish to flee and evade, that to make a detour around life's obstacles and to escape meeting its problems is, in the end, unprofitable. He knows that his wisdom must arise out of the fullness and not out of the poverty of experience and that it is no use non-co-operatively shirking the world's struggle, for it is largely through such struggle that he can bring forth his own latent resources. Philosophy does not refuse to face life, however tragic or however frightful it may be, and uses such experiences to profit its own higher purpose.

XIII.20.166

It is most important to get rid of an unbalanced condition. Most people are in such a condition although few know it. For example, intellectuality without spirituality is human paralysis. No man should submit to such suicidal conditions. All men should seek and achieve integrality. To be wrapped up in a single side of life or to be overactive in a single direction ends by making a man mildly insane in the true and not technical sense of this word. The remedy is to tone down here and built up there, to cultivate the neglected sides, and especially to cultivate the opposite side. Admittedly, it is extremely difficult for most of us, circumstanced as we usually are, to achieve a perfect development and equal balance of all the sides. But this is no excuse for accepting conditions completely as they are and making no effort at all to remedy them. The difficulty for many aspirants in attaining such an admirably balanced character lies in their tendency to be obsessed by a particular technique which they followed in former births but which cannot by itself meet with the very different conditions of today. We must counterbalance the habit of living only in a part of our being. When we have become harmoniously balanced in the philosophic sense, heart and head will work together to answer the same question, the unhurrying sense of eternity and the pressing urge of the hour will combine to make decisions as wise as they are practical, and the transcendental intuitions will suggest or confirm the workings of reason. In this completed integral life, thought and action, devotion and knowledge do not wrestle against each other but become one. Such is the triune quest of intelligence, aspiration, and action.

XIII.19.35

The first question is also the final one; it is quite short, quite simple, and yet it is also the most important question which anyone could ever ask, whether of himself or of others. This question is: 'What is consciousness?' Whoever traces the answer through all its levels will find himself in the end in the very presence of the universal consciousness otherwise called God.

XIV.22.105

If a man asks why he can find no trace of God's presence in himself, I answer that he is full of evidence, not merely traces. God is present in him as consciousness, the state of being aware; as thought, the capacity to think; as activity, the power to move; and as stillness, the condition of ego, emotion, intellect, and body which finally and clearly reveals what these other things simply point to. 'Be still, and know that I am God' is a statement of being whose truth can be tested by experiment and whose value can be demonstrated by experience.

XIII.21.120

Think of yourself as the individual and you are sure to die; think of yourself as the universal and you enter deathlessness, for the universal is always and eternally there. We know no beginning and no ending to the cosmic process. Its being IS: we can say no more. Be that rather than this—that which is as infinite and homeless as space, that which is timeless and unbroken. Take the whole of life as your own being. Do not divorce, do not separate yourself from it. It is the hardest of tasks for it demands that we see our own relative insignificance amid this infinite and vast process. The change that is needed is entirely a mental one. Change your outlook and with it 'heaven will be added unto you'.

XIV.22.137

The principle which makes union with the Overself possible is always the same, albeit on different levels. Whether it appears as humility in prayer, passivity to intuition, stillness in meditation, or serenity despite untoward circumstances, these attitudes temporarily weaken the ego and lessen its domination. They temporarily silence the ego and give the Overself the opportunity to touch us or work through us. So long as the ego dominates us, we are outside the reach of the Overself and separated from its help.

XV.24.13

He is happy even though he has no blessed consciousness of the Overself, no transcendental knowledge of it, but only secondhand news about it. Why, then, is he happy? Because he knows that he has found the way to both consciousness and knowledge. He is content to wait, working nevertheless as he waits; for if he remains faithful to the quest, what other result can there be than attainment? Even if he has to wait fifty years or fifty lifetimes, he will and must gain it.

XIV.22.108

There is only one way to settle his question of whether the Overself exists and that is the very way most moderns refuse to accept. Each must gain for himself the *authentic* mystical experience. Sugar can really be known only by its sweet taste, the Overself only by opening the doors of the mind to consciousness of its presence.

XV.24.14-15

If the divine presence is dwelling at the core of his mind, then the divine bliss, peace, and strength are dwelling at the core of his mind too. Why then should he let outward troubles rob him of the chance to share them? Why should he let only the troubles enter his consciousness, and withdraw all attention from the bliss and peace and strength? The conditions of this world are subject to the cosmic law of change. They are temporary. But the bright core within him is not. Why then give a permanent meaning to those conditions by a total surrender to the sadness they cause?

XIV.22.239

If he were pure enough and prepared enough to receive the

light in all its fullness and in all the parts of his being, the glimpse would not leave him. But he is not.

XV.23.161

Concentrate on the remembered delight, the lovely silence, of some past glimpse. Try to bring it into sharp vivid focus.

XIII.20.235-6

From all these studies, meditations, and actions the student will little by little emerge an inwardly changed man. He comes to the habitual contemplation of his co-partnership with the universe as a whole, to the recognition that personal isolation is illusory, and thus takes the firm steps on the ultimate path towards becoming a true philosopher. The realization of the hidden unity of his own life with the life of the whole world manifests finally in infinite compassion for all living things. Thus he learns to subdue the personal will to the cosmic one, narrow selfish affection to the wide-spreading desire for the common welfare. Compassion comes to full blossom in his heart like a lotus flower in the sunshine. From this lofty standpoint, he no longer regards mankind as being those whom he unselfishly serves but rather as being those who give him the opportunity to serve. He will suddenly or slowly experience an emotional exaltation culminating in an utter change of heart. Its course will be marked by a profound reorientation of feeling toward his fellow creatures. The fundamental egoism which in open or masked forms has hitherto motivated him will be abandoned: the noble altruism which has hitherto seemed an impractical and impossible ideal, will become practicable and possible. For a profound sympathy to all other beings will dwell in his heart. Never again will it be possible for him wilfully to injure another; but on the contrary the welfare of the All will become his concern. In Jesus' words he is 'born again'. He will find his highest happiness, after seeking reality and truth, in seeking the welfare of all other beings alongside of his own. The practical consequence of this is that he will be inevitably led to incessant effort for their service and enlightenment. He will not merely echo the divine will but will allow it actively to work within him. And with the thought comes the power to do so, the grace of the Overself to help him to achieve quickly what the Underself cannot achieve. In the service of others he can partially forget his loss of trance-joy and know that the liberated self which he had experienced in interior meditation must be equated by the expanded self in altruistic action.

XV.24.71-2

If he can act attentively and yet stand aside from the results of his actions; if he can discharge his responsibilities or carry out his duties without being swept into elation by success or into misery by failure; if he can move in the world, enjoy its pleasures and endure its pains, and yet hold unwaveringly to the quest of what transcends the world, then he has become what the Indians call a 'karma yogi' and what the Greeks call a 'man'.

XIII.20.219-21

Life is not a matter of meditation methods exclusively. Their study and practice is necessary, but let them be put in their proper place. Both mystical union and metaphysical understanding are necessary steps on this quest, because it is only from them that the student can mount to the still higher grade of universal being represented by the sage. For we not only need psychological exercises to train the inner being, but also psychological exercises to train the point of view. But the student must not stay in mysticism as he must not stay in metaphysics. In both cases he should take all that they have to give him but struggle through and come out on the other side. For the mysticism of emotion is not the shrine where Isis dwells but only the vestibule to the shrine, and the metaphysician who can only see in reason the supreme faculty of man has not reflected enough. Let him go farther and he shall find that its own supreme achievement is to point beyond itself to that principle or Mind whence it takes its rise. Mysticism needs the check of philosophic discipline. Metaphysics needs the vivification of mystical meditation. Both must bear fruit in inspired action or they are but half-born. In no other way than through acts can they rise to the lofty status of facts.

The realization of what man is here for is the realization of a fused and unified life wherein all the elements of action, feeling, and thought are vigorously present. It is not, contrary to the beliefs of mystics, a condition of profound entrancement alone, nor, contrary to the reasonings of metaphysicians, a condition of intellectual clarity alone, and still less, contrary to the opinions of theologians, a condition of complete faith in God alone. We are here to live, which means to think, feel, and act also. We have not only to curb thought in meditation, but also to whip it in reflection. We have not only to control emotion in self-discipline, but also to release it in laughter, relaxation, affection, and pleasure. We have not only to perceive the transiency and illusion of material existence, but also to work, serve, strive, and move strenuously and thus justify physical existence. We have to learn that when we look at what we really are we stand alone in the awed solitude of the Overself, but when we look at where we now are we see not isolated individuals but members of a thronging human community. The hallmark of a living man, therefore, ought to be an integral and inseparable activity of heart, head, and hand, itself occurring within the mysterious stillness and silence of its inspirer, the Overself.

The mistake of the lower mystic is when he would set up a final goal in meditation itself, when he would stop at the 'letting-go' of the external world which is quite properly an essential process of mysticism, and when he would let his reasoning faculty fall into a permanent stupor merely because it is right to do so during the moments of mental quiet. When, however, he learns to understand that the antinomy of meditation and action belongs only to an intermediate stage of this quest, when he comes later to the comprehension that detachment from the world is only to be sought to enable him to move with perfect freedom amid the things of the world and not to flee them, and when he perceives at long last that the reason itself is God-given to safeguard his journey and later to bring his realization into self-consciousness—then he shall have travelled from the second to the third degree in this freemasonry of ultimate wisdom. For that which had earlier hindered his advance now helps it; such is the paradox which he must unravel if he would elevate himself from the satisfactions of mysticism to the perceptions of philosophy. If his meditations once estranged him from the world, now they bring him closer to it! If formerly he could find God only within himself, now he can find nothing else that is not God! He has advanced from the chrysalis-state of x to the butterfly state of y.

If there be any worth in this teaching, such lies in its equal appeal to experience and to reason. For that inward beatitude which it finally brings is superior to any other that mundane man has felt and, bereft of all violent emotion itself though it be, paradoxically casts all violent emotions of joy in the shade. When we comprehend that this teaching establishes as fact what the subtlest reasoning points to in theory, reveals in man's own life the presence of that Overself which reflection discovers as from a remote distance, we know that here at long last is something fit for a modern man. The agitations of the heart and the troublings of the head take their dying breaths.

2

THE TEACHER

XVI.25.102

There are noteworthy differences between the genuine illuminate and the false one. But I shall indicate only a few of the points one may observe in the man who is truly self-realized. First of all, he does not desire to become the leader of a new cult; therefore, he does not indulge in any of the attempts to draw publicity or notice which mark our modern saviours. He never seeks to arouse attention by oddity of teaching, talk, dress, or manner. In fact, he does not even desire to appear as a teacher, seeks no adherents, and asks no pupils to join him. Though he possesses immense spiritual power which may irresistibly influence your life, he will seem quite unconscious of it. He makes no claim to the possession of peculiar powers. He is completely without pose or pretence. The things which arouse passion or love or hatred in men do not seem to touch him; he is indifferent to them as Nature is to our comments when we praise her sunshine or revile her storms. For in him, we have to recognize a man freed, loosed from every limit which desire and emotion can place upon us. He walks detached from the anxious thoughts or seductive passions which eat out the hearts of men. Though he behaves and lives simply and naturally, we are aware that there is a mystery within that man. We are unable to avoid the impression that because his understanding has plumbed life deeper than other men's, we are compelled to call a halt when we would attempt to comprehend him.

XII.18.105

The translator into German of *The Wisdom of the Overself* went
to Egypt for a three-week rest to avoid nervous collapse after
the death of a most beloved person, who she believed was
her twin soul. While she was staying at a hotel in Luxor, various shoeshine men came there and sat outside, offering their
services to guests. One day an elderly Arab appeared among
them, with a striking face and an even more striking radiation of tranquillity. She was so drawn to him that she let him
polish her shoes in preference to the one who usually did
them. When he finished she paid him four piasters (which
was double the normal payment), because she felt so com-
forted by his presence. He immediately returned half the
money to her saying, 'The Lord will look after the needs of
tomorrow. Two piasters are enough for today.' He never
came again to the hotel, but she constantly thought of him
and his peace, to have something to save her from utter
despair. After she had returned to Europe still grieving and
depressed, he appeared to her in a dream surrounded by light
and blessed her. When she awoke, his mental image still
seemed to be there, but it said, 'This is the last time I shall
come to you. From now on you must take care of yourself.'
He never reappeared, but she slowly recovered thereafter.

XV.24.47

As I was studying him one wintry evening in the snow-
covered streets of St Albans where I first met him, strange
thoughts filled my head. Under those tattered rags dwelled
a spirit of purest sapphire. The inscrutable writ of destiny
had put him upon this path. But as he spoke to me, in calm
happy tones, of diverse spiritual matters, I felt my mind being
steadily raised by the tremendous power of his dynamic
thoughts to a sublimer state. I sensed his amazing peace, his
godlike realization, his cosmic outlook, his profoundly
impersonal feeling, and I knew that the man before me would
not willingly change his lot for that of any millionaire on
earth. Hard to understand, this, but there are a few who will
grasp my meaning. I do not preach poverty as a path to

peace. But I do say that unless you have found *inner* wealth, unless your success exists within your heart and thoughts and conscience also, the external symbol of an all-powerful cheque book is a mockery and may even prove a curse as well.

XV.24.102

We are vocally benumbed on entering the presence of embodied spiritual attainment, for the intellect is silent and abashed at feeling so acutely its own inferiority, its own futility. And it is the intellect in which we mostly live, not the intuition.

XII.18.106

No Maharishee, no Aurobindo, no Saint Francis can save you. It is the Holy Spirit which saves man by its Grace. The ministrations of these men may kindle faith and quiet the mind, may help you to prepare the right conditions and offer a focus for your concentration, but they offer no guarantee of salvation. It is highly important not to forget this, not to deify man and neglect the true God who must come to you directly and act upon you directly.

XI.16.131

The childish worship of every illumined man as if he were the World-Mind itself and the blind reception of his every utterance as if it were sacrosanct—these are defects to be regretted. And they occur not only among the Orientals, where it is to be expected, but also among the increasing number of those Occidentals who accept the doctrine of the Orientals and imitate their attitudes. They point to excessive attachment to the limited personality of their spiritual leader, so that it is disproportionate to the pure impersonal Spirit of which he is but the channel. They reveal the devotee to be on the religio-mystical level, to have advanced beyond popular religion but not to have travelled sufficiently far into mysticism proper to feel comfortable there. He has escaped from the crowd which is taken in by the mere outward forms of religious observance, but he cannot yet escape from the olden habit or need of depending on some outward thing or person. So, he transfers to his master's body the devotion he formerly gave to popular pieties.

XI.16.154

It is unfortunate that the printed page democratically levels all alike; that it puts on terms of a flat plane of equality the vital convincing speech of a Jesus with the speech of a nonentity; that it invests a man or an idea with a dignity which in actuality they may not at all possess; that all words when set in type look more or less equally imposing and important, no matter by whose lips they are spoken or by whose hand they are written. Were we all gifted with profounder mental percipiency, the fool in philosopher's clothing would then be plainly revealed for what he is; the scratcher of Truth's surface would no longer be able to bawl successfully that he had solved the secrets of the universe; and even the brainless idiot who stumbles on a momentary ecstasy would not be able to assert to an admiring audience of devotees that he had become a Master. Then, too, we would be able to penetrate the disguises of some humble ones and raise them high up on the pedestals of respect which they deserve; we would bend the knee in reverence before the figures of those who really do possess truth but do not possess the gift for personal publicity, who know the Infinite reality but who know not how to turn it to finite profit.

XI.16.119

Just as the true teacher will widen the circle of a student's mental contacts, so the false one will plunge him in intellectual isolation, will keep him wholly under his own influence and prevent the enrichment of ideas and expansion of outlook necessary to his progress.

XI.16.120

A true teacher does not want to direct anyone's life. He may offer suggestions but he would never insist on their being carried out.

XI.16.182

Because a man has had some kind of inner revelation it does not follow that everything in life and the universe has become plain to him and that he has become a kind of human encyclopaedia.

XI.16.316

It may be distressing to those who have full faith in the revelations of seers and ardent devotion for them to learn that these revelations may not always be what their receivers believe them to be, that they may not be sacred at all, but only human, or partly sacred and partly human. They may be even deceptive, mistaken, or imaginary. Those who know nothing of the controversies which agitate mystical circles may regret this statement but it would be easy to document it fully. But such remarks do not apply to *philosophic* insight, its personalities and tenets. Its entire approach and method are sufficiently protected against aberrations to avoid them. For philosophy insists on asking—and finding the answer to—the question: 'What is it that seers attain during their highest meditation? Is it their own imagination, their own idea, or is it truth and reality?'

XIV.22.225

The question whether someone is a mystic or yogi can be answered easily enough once we understand what is his state of consciousness and what the mystical condition really is. All the annals of the vanished past and all the experiences of the living present inform us that whoever enters into it feels his natural egotism subside, his fierce passions assuaged, his restless thoughts stilled, his troubled emotions pacified, his habitual world-view spiritualized, and his whole person caught up into a beatific supernal power. Did he ever have this kind of consciousness? His words and deeds, his personal presence and psychological self-betrayal should pro-

claim with a united voice what he is. No man who habitually enters such a blessed state could ever bring himself to
hate or injure a fellow human being.

II.16.316

I honour and revere these saints. It is good for us that such
men have been on earth. Nevertheless, man cannot perfect
himself *in* this world although he must do so *through* this
world. Hence we must grant the fact that the greatest
teachers of the race were human, after all, and therefore subject to human limitations. They did not cease to be human
beings merely because they became spiritual geniuses. If their
declarations reveal the heights above, they also reflect the
plains below. Respectful courteous criticism in my own private notebooks, to clarify my ideas of their theoretical standpoint and practical attitude for the purposes of elucidating
the truth, is allowable. This is different from public denun-
ciation in print. Where is the alleged resemblance of doctrine and unity of spirit among the different mystical schools
really to be found? The contradictions and even oppositions
are as numerous as the similarities and harmonies. If this
means anything, it means that mystics do colour their perception with their individual characteristics, however much
they may claim to be above the ego. It means, too, that such
colouration is most often effected quite unconsciously. The
white light of the pure experience is always coloured by
prepossessions or emotions, and always suffers from the
change.

XI.16.188

Whereas St Thomas Aquinas stopped writing his books when
the inner experience came to him, Shankaracharya started
writing his own. Thus one and the same kind of spiritual
consciousness illuminating two different kinds of mind
brought about two different and opposite decisions! What
does this show? That the human mind *does* colour the revelation's reception or its communication.

XI.16.296

Those to whom the higher power has to reveal itself through visions seen clairvoyantly, or sounds heard clairaudiently, or teachings impressed mentally are helped in this inferior way only because they lack the capacity to receive in a superior way. And this remains just as true if the vision is of their most respected Spiritual Leader, the sound none other than the mystic Sanskrit syllable OM, and the teaching fully descriptive of the seven planes of progressive being. If they had possessed the capacity to receive by pure insight without any reference to the method by which we receive through the agency of five bodily senses and the intellect, they would not have needed such occult experiences, which are in a sense semi-materialistic. Only when these agents are stilled, and the image-making faculty silenced, and the time or place lost, is pure Spirit known. Not only must the body and its activities, the intellect and its movements be forgotten, but even their representation in an occult or psychical manner must be absent. It is then only that there can be true identity with the Overself. All other experiences are mere projections going *out* from it, and hence involved in references to the ego.

XI.16.316

A true inspiration communicating a true revelation must still find a perfectly ego-free mind through which to operate, if there is to be publication to others in any way through spoken or written words.

XVI.25.194

The true adept does not sell either the secrets of his knowledge or the use of his powers. There are several reasons for this. The most important is that he would harm himself for he would lose the link with the very source of his knowledge and power. He does not possess them in himself but by virtue of being possessed by the Higher Self. From the moment that he attempted to make them a means of worldly profit, It would gradually begin to desert him. Another reason is that he would lose his privileged position to speak the pure truth. To the extent that he had to rely upon purchasers of it, to that extent he would have to shape it or conform it to their tastes and prejudices; otherwise they would refuse to have it. He would have to use his powers to please them. He would have to accommodate his knowledge to their weaknesses. He could succeed in the profession of teaching truth only by failing in his own duty of realizing truth. For the truth, being the one thing he got without price, is the one thing which he must give without price. This the law governing its distribution. Anyone who violates it proves by this very violation that he does not possess truth in all its shining purity.

XVI.25.223-5

We are asked why, if thought-transference be a fact, the hibernating hermit should not still represent the loftiest achievement, should not in fact be as antisocial as he superficially seems. He may be hidden away in a mountain cave, but is not his mind free to roam where it likes and has not its power been raised to a supreme degree by his mystical practices? We reply that if he is merely concerned with resting in his inner tranquillity undisturbed by the thought of others, then his achievement is only a self-centred one.

There is much confusion amongst students about these yogis who are supposed to sit in solitude and help humanity telepathically. It is not only yogis who sit in solitude who are doing so. Nor is it needful to be a solitary to be able to do so. The truth is that most yogis who live in solitude are still in the student stage, still trying to develop themselves. And even in the rarer cases where a yogi has perfected himself in meditation, he may be using the latter simply to bask egotistically in inner peace for his own benefit and without a thought for others. It is only when a man is a philosophic yogi that he will be deliberately using his meditational self-absorptions to uplift individuals and help humanity for their good. If the mystic *is* using his mental powers for altruistic ends, if he *is* engaged in telepathically helping others at a distance, then he has gone beyond the ordinary mystical level and we salute him for it.

The Adept will not try to influence any other man, much less try to control him. Therefore, his notion of serving another by enlightening him does not include the activity of proselytizing, but rather the office of teaching. Such service means helping a man to understand for himself and to see for himself what he could not see and understand before. The Adept does this not only by using the ordinary methods of speech, writing, and example, but much more by an extraordinary method which only an Adept can employ. In this he puts himself in a passive attitude towards the other person's ego and thus registers the character, thought, and feeling in one swift general impression, which manifests itself within his own consciousness like a photograph upon a sensitized film. He recognizes this as a picture of the evolutionary degree to which the other person has attained, but he recognizes it also as a picture of the false self with which the other person identifies himself. No matter how much sympathy he feels for the other man, no matter how negative are the emotions or the thoughts he finds reproducing themselves within his own being, it is without effect upon himself. This is because he has outgrown both the desires and the illusions which still reign over the other man's mind. With the next step in his technique he challenges that self as being fearful for its own unworthy and ultimately doomed existence, and finally dismisses the picture of it in favour of the person's true self, the divine Overself. Then he throws out of his mind every thought of the other person's imperfect egoistic condition and replaces it by the affirmation of his true spiritual selfhood.

Thus, if the Adept begins his service to another who attracted by his wisdom seeks counselling or by his godliness seeks his inspiration, by noting the defects in the character of the person, he ends it by ignoring them. He then images the seeker as standing serenely in the light, free from the ego and its desires, strong and wise and pure because living in the truth. The Adept closes his eyes to the present state of the seeker, to all the evidences of distress and weakness and darkness which he earlier noted, and opens them to the real, innermost state of the seeker, where he sees him united with the Overself. He persists in silently holding this thought and this picture, and he holds it with the dynamic intensity of which he only is capable. The effect of this inner working sometimes appears immediately in the seeker's consciousness, but more likely it will take some time to rise up from the subconscious mind. Even if it takes years to manifest itself, it will certainly do so in the end.

We know that one mind can influence another through the medium of speech or writing: we know also that it may even influence another directly and without any medium through the silent power of telepathy. All this work takes place on the level of thought and emotion. But the Adept may not only work on this level: it is possible for him to work on a still deeper level. He can go into the innermost core of his own being and there touch the innermost core of the other man's being. In this way, Spirit speaks to Spirit, but without words or even thoughts. Within his innermost being there is a mysterious emptiness to which the Adept alone gains access during meditation or trance. All thoughts die at its threshold as he enters it. But when eventually he returns to the ordinary state and the thinking activity starts again, then those first series of thoughts are endowed with a peculiar power, are impregnated with a magical potency. Their echoes reverberate telepathically across space in the minds of others to whom they may be directed deliberately by the Adept. Their influence upon sympathetic and responsive persons is at first too subtle and too deep to be recognized, but eventually they reach the surface of consciousness.

This indeed is the scientific fact behind the popular medieval European and contemporary Oriental belief in the virtue of an Adept's blessing and the value of an Adept's initiation. The Adept's true perception of him is somewhere registered like a seed in the subconscious mind of the receptive person, and will in the course of time work its way up through the earth of the unconscious like a plant until it appears above ground in the conscious mind. If it is much slower in showing its effects, it is also much more effectual, much more lasting than the ordinary way of communicating thought or transmitting influence. In this way, by his own inner growth he will begin to perceive, little by little, for himself the truth about his own inner being and outer life in the same way that the Adept perceives it. This is nothing less than a passage from the ego's point of view to the higher one.

VIII.12.70

Angkor Wat: The chief sanctuary on the third (top) floor of the temple. I squatted several paces in front of the shrine where a standing gold lacquered Buddha was positioned with one hand raised in a world-blessing. At his feet reclined another statue, the dying Buddha (unpainted), with one hand under his head and behind him three small bodhisattvas paying respectful homage to their master. Very soon, lulled by the peace of the sanctuary and sensitive to its extraordinary subtle power, I unified myself with that Buddha. My gaze was fixed across the intervening paved floor and doorless doorway, unfaltering, upon the eyes of the standing Buddha, the others being shrouded in the darkness of that small room. We became ONE. A spiritual current passed perceptibly from the mysterious figure into my squatting cross-legged body. In those divine moments before sunfall, when a sublime inner detachment and peace had engulfed me, I knew that I had got from Angkor Wat that which I have travelled over many leagues to get.

XVI.25.233-41

It is rarely understood here in the Occident that where spiritual help is given telepathically, it is given as a general inspiration to remember the divine laws, to have faith in them, and to follow the higher ideals. It is not given as a particular guidance in the detailed application of those laws, nor in the day to day outworking of those ideals. The teacher gives by radiation from his inner life and being, and the disciple draws it into his own mind by a correct approach and mental attitude towards the teacher. What he receives, however, is impersonal. His own ego will have to convert it into a personal form and will have to apply the ideals instilled into him. Another misconception is also very common: 'Is it not the master himself who helps me at such moments?' is a question asked in astonished surprise by those disciples who feel his presence keenly, see his image vividly, and converse with him personally in experiences which are genuinely telepathic in character. The answer is that it both is and is not the master himself. The minute particulars of the pictorial experience, or the actual words of a message are supplied by the disciple's own ego. The mental inspiration and moral exaltation derived from it and the emotional peace which surround it are drawn telepathically out of the master's being. Both these elements are so commingled and diffused with one another in the disciple's mind, and so instantaneously too, that inevitably he gets only an unclear and partial understanding of his experience. The truth is that the master does not necessarily have to be conscious of the pupil's telepathic call for help in order to make that help available. Nor does he personally have to do anything about it in order to ensure that his help is transmitted. Just as it is said that the cow's idea of heaven is of a place eternally filled with grass, and that a man's idea of God is a magnified human being, so it may be said that the uninformed aspirant's idea of a spiritual guide is often only an improved and enlarged version of himself. The master is pictured as being filled with oozing sentimentality, however pious, vibrating with personal emotion, and fluttered by his disciple's changes of fortune—as being almost always on the verge of tears with sympathy for others, as fretting over every little fault and change of mood in his disciples every hour of the twenty-four, every day of the week, every week of the year. It is imagined that the master seeks only to influence pleasurable experiences towards his disciples and to divert painful ones—as though pleasurableness were the only good and pain the only evil. It is easy for people to open the doors of a weak sentiment or to gild the bars of the cage of selfishness and forget the living prisoner within. To them the

Illuminate is a paradox of conduct. For the same law which stays his hand from giving promiscuous relief also bids him render unto each man his due.

But it is for the pupil himself to cultivate perfect poise between the two extremes of utter dependence upon a teacher and complete reliance upon himself. Both extremes will obstruct his advance upon this path. Nor will it be enough to find the mid-way point between them and adhere always to that point. The definition of poise will vary at different stages of his career. At one time it will be absolutely necessary for him to cultivate self-reliance, whereas a couple of years later it may be equally necessary to cultivate a mood of dependence. What is proper at one time or period may not be proper at another. Which phase is to be uppermost or when both are to be perfectly balanced is something which can be decided only by a mingling of inner prompting, logical reflection, and other circumstances.

'To the real enquirers after knowledge, the master's words will enable one to know his own self. A teacher's Grace, if it becomes *en rapport* with his disciple, will of itself in a mysterious manner enable the disciple to perceive directly the Brahmic principle within. It is impossible for the disciple to understand how Brahman is prior to his direct perception. It is indeed very rare to attain that state without the help of a Guru.'—*Yoga Vasistha*.

The difference between a false teacher and a genuine one is often the difference between a dominating dictator and a quiet guide. The false teacher will seek to emasculate your will or even to enslave your mind, whereas the true teacher will endeavour to exalt you into a sense of your own self-responsibility. The teacher who demands or accepts such servility is dangerous to true growth. In the end, he will require a loyalty which should be given only to the Overself. The true teacher will carry your soul into greater freedom and not less, into stabilizing truth and not emotional moods. The true teacher has no desire to hold anyone in pupilage, but on the contrary gladly welcomes the time when the disciple is able to stand without help from outside.

But because talk is easy and redemption is not demanded except in the distant future, these false teachers thrive for a while. Many of them are but students, yet find it hard to take the low places where humility dwells. Hence their gravity; hence the laughter of the gods at them. Could they but laugh at themselves awhile, and perhaps at their doctrines occasionally, they might regain balance, a sense of proportion—but greatest of all true Humility. They are not necessarily deliberate misleaders of others, these self-appointed saviours, but their mystical experiences have given them false impressions about themselves. Their authority is fallible and their doctrines are false. They find it easy to deliver themselves of lofty teachings, but hard to put the same teaching into practice. These gurus promise much, but in the sequel do not redeem their word. These self-styled adepts appear to be adepts in circumlocution more than in anything else.

Those who openly court worship or secretly exult in it cannot possibly have entered into the true Kingdom of Heaven. For the humility it demands is aptly described by Jesus when he describes its entrance as smaller than a needle's eye.

Would-be disciples who are so eager to fill this role that they are swept straightaway into enthusiasm by the extravagant promises of would-be masters, usually lack both the desire and the competence to investigate the qualifications of such masters. Consequently they pay the penalty of their lack of discrimination.

If a nation accepts and follows a wicked man as its leader, then there must be some fault in it which made this possible. And if a seeker accepts a false guide on his spiritual path, then there must be some false intuition, false thinking, or false standards which made this possible too.

There are various ways of appraising a teacher at his true worth. We may watch his external life and notice how he conducts his affairs, how he talks and works, and how he behaves towards other men. Or we may dive deep into his interior nature and plumb the depths of his mental life. The latter course presupposes some degree of psychic sensitive-

ness. The best way is to combine both, to penetrate the
unseen and to observe the visible.

Nanak, founder of the Sikh faith, uttered this warning:
'Do not reverence those who call themselves guru and who
beg for alms. Only those who live by the fruits of their labour
and do honest and useful work are in the way of truth.'

The ideal sage is not the wandering *sadhu* but the working
one, he who works incessantly to relieve the sufferings of
his fellows and to enlighten them.

There are too many aspirants who are hoping, like Micaw-
ber in Dickens' story, for something to turn up. In their case
it is a spiritual master who will not only take their burdens
and responsibilities off their shoulders but, much more, translate them overnight into a realm of spiritual consciousness
for ever more. They go on waiting and they go on hoping,
but nothing turns up and no one appears. What is the reason for this frustration of their hopes? It is that they fail to
work while they wait, fail to prepare themselves to be fit
for such a meeting, fail to recognize that whether they have
a master or not they must still work upon themselves dili-
gently, and that the harder they work in this task of self-
improvement, the more likely it is that they will find a master.
They are like children who want to be carried all the way
and coddled while they are being carried. They are waiting
for someone to do what they ought to be doing for themselves. They are waiting to receive from outside what they
could start getting straightaway by delving inside themselves.

Because of bad karma and inherent insensitivity most
people fail to recognize the master as such, and therefore
fail to take advantage of the opportunity offered by his
presence among them.

Only the master's body can be perceived by the physical
senses. His spirit must be received by intuition. If acceptance
or rejection of him is based on the physical senses alone, then
only a false master will be found, never a true one. If the
idea of him is predetermined by conceptions about his
appearance, and if he is accepted only because he looks hand-
some or speaks well, and rejected because he is lame, blind,

or diseased, then the true masters will never be found, only charlatans and imposters.

He who says, 'I want no mediator between myself and Truth,' has the right instinct but the wrong attitude. None save self can make the divine discovery for him, but this is not to say that an adept who has attained the inward light cannot come to the one stumbling in darkness and give a guiding hand. As a matter of fact the true teacher does much more than this. He even gives that stimulus which carries us over the quest so steep and difficult, so beset with snares, and so often clouded over that a guide who has travelled the path already is more necessary than we dream. It is he who points out the direction when all are uncertain, who encourages when our pace slackens, who strengthens when our will weakens, and who becomes a bridge as it were between our present standpoint and a diviner one.

The oracle of wisdom must find a seat, the stream of divinity must find an outlet. Hence the need for a teacher.

If it be asked, are the great Adepts accessible by the masses and willing to bestow help upon them, the answer is that they are not. They leave the masses to the infallible workings of gross Nature, which influences and develops them by its general internal evolutionary impetus; they leave even ordinary aspirants to the guidance of more advanced ones. In one way they stand like helpless spectators of the Great Show, for they may not interfere with but must ever respect the freewill of others, whose experience of embodied life is regarded by them as sacred. For this experience incarnation is taken, and its lessons are a fruit of which not even the Adepts may rob any man or woman. They reveal themselves to, and shed their aid upon, the few who can win their own way to their presence by preparatory self-purification, mystical methods, and philosophic understanding. Their duty is to guide such as have earned the right to their guidance and who can inwardly respond to them. From the foregoing statements it should now be obvious that the teachers who accept any and every applicant, themselves belong to the lowest rung and possess an imperfect character.

There is a craze for Messianic revelations. The weak and

credulous will always worship the bold. Hence any man who has seen a corner of the veil lifted can come forward as a god who has seen all the veil lifted, and he is sure to collect an obedient flock. Such men are very apt at creating personal fantasies. They appear in their own eyes as God-sent guides and liberators.

It is a strange but saddening thought that all these would-be Christs are conscious of a world-wide mission which they have to perform, whereas the real adept is unconscious of having any mission whatever. The Infinite is embodied in him and carries out its work perfectly without calling up his own separate ego-hood. Since the latter has been blown out like a candle he cannot be conscious of having a mission. Only those who are still under the delusion of separateness can harbour such an idea.

The conclusion is that instead of wandering about looking for Christs to come, we should be better employed wandering inward looking for the Christ there, the Christ within. Such a truth is our best Saviour and the surest Avatar of our time.

XVI.25.242

In an adept's presence, as in the sun's presence, things begin to happen of their own accord. People feel a spiritual quickening and begin to call him master and themselves disciples. The whole institution of discipleship is nothing but a convenient illusion created by people themselves and tolerantly permitted by the adept for their sakes. He himself, however, is aware of no such thing, has no favouritism, but sends out his light and power to the whole of mankind indiscriminately. Yet this is not to say that the disciples' illusion is a useless or baseless one. It is indeed very real from their standpoint and experience and affords the greatest help to their advancement. Ultimately, however, towards the final stages of the path, they discover him entirely within themselves as the infinite reality, not disparate from themselves, and the sense of duality begins to disappear. Later they merge in him and 'I and my Father are one' may then be truly uttered.

3

FROM MYSTICISM TO PHILOSOPHY

XIII.20.5-6

People sometimes ask me to what religion I belong or to what school of yoga I adhere. If I answer them, which is not often, I tell them: 'To none and to all!' If such a paradox annoys them, I try to soften their wrath by adding that I am a student of philosophy. During my journeys to the heavenly realms of infinite eternal and absolute existence, I did not once discover any labels marked Christian, Hindu, Catholic, Protestant, Zen, Shin, Platonist, Hegelian, and so on, any more than I discovered labels marked Englishman, American, or Hottentot. All such ascriptions would contradict the very nature of the ascriptionless existence. All sectarian differences are merely intellectual ones. They have no place in that level which is deeper than intellectual function. They divide men into hostile groups only because they are pseudo-spiritual. He who has tasted of the pure Spirit's own freedom will be unwilling to submit himself to the restrictions of cult and creed. Therefore I could not conscientiously affix a label to my own outlook or to the teaching about this existence which I have embraced. In my secret heart I separate myself from nobody, just as this teaching itself excludes no other in its perfect comprehension. Because I had to call it by some name as soon as I began to write about it, I called it philosophy because this is too wide and too general a name to become the property of any single sect. In doing so I merely returned to its ancient and noble meaning among the Greeks who, in the Eleusinian Mysteries, designated the spiritual truth learned at initiation as 'philosophy' and the initiate himself as 'philosopher' or lover of wisdom.

Now genuine wisdom, being in its higher phase the fruit of a transcendental insight, is sublimely dateless and unchangeable. Yet its mode of expression is necessarily dated and may therefore change. Perhaps this pioneering attempt to fill the term 'philosophy' with a content which combines ancient tradition with modern innovation will help the few who are sick of intellectual intolerances that masquerade as spiritual insight. Perhaps it may free such broader souls from the need of adopting a separative standpoint with all the frictions, prejudices, egotisms, and hatreds which go with it, and afford them an intellectual basis for practising a profound compassion for all alike. It it as natural for those reared on limited conceptions of life to limit their faith and loyalty to a particular group or a particular area of this planet as it is natural for those reared on philosophic truth to widen their vision and service into world-comprehension and world-fellowship. The philosopher's larger and nobler vision refuses to establish a separate group consciousness for himself and for those who think as he does. Hence he refuses to establish a new cult, a new association, or a new label. To him the oneness of mankind is a fact and not a fable. He is always conscious of the fact that he is a citizen of the world-community. While acknowledging the place and need of lesser loyalties for unphilosophical persons, he cannot outrage truth by confining his own self solely to such loyalties.

Why this eagerness to separate ourselves from the rest of mankind and collect into a sect, to wear a new label that proclaims difference and division? The more we believe in the oneness of life, the less we ought to herd ourselves behind barriers. To add a new cult to the existing list is to multiply the causes of human division and thence of human strife. Let those of us who can do so be done with this seeking of ever-new disunity, this fostering of ever-fresh prejudices, and let those who cannot do so keep it at least as an ideal—however remote and however far-off its attainment may seem—for after all it is ultimate direction and not immediate position that matters most. The democratic abolishment of class status and exclusive groups, which will be a distinctive feature of the coming age, should also show itself in the circles of mystical and philosophic students. If they have any superiority over others, let them display it by a superiority of conduct grounded in a diviner consciousness. Nevertheless, with all the best will in the world to refrain from starting a new group, the distinctive character of their conduct and the unique character of their outlook will, of themselves, mark out the followers of such teaching. Therefore whatever metaphysical unity with others may be perceived and whatever inward willingness to identify interests with them may be felt, some kind of practical indication of its goal and outward particularization of its path will necessarily and inescapably arise of their own accord. And I do not know of any better or broader name with which to mark those who pursue this quest than to say that they are students of philosophy.

XIII.20.7

We may generally distinguish three different views of the world. The first is that which comes easily and naturally and it depends on five-sense experience alone. It may be called materialism, and may take various shapes. The second is religious in its elementary state, depending on faith, and mystical in its higher stage, depending on intuition and transcendental experience. The third is scientific in its elementary state, depending on concrete reason, and metaphysical in its higher state, depending on abstract reason. Although these are the views generally held amongst men, they do not exhaust the possibilities of human intelligence. There is a fourth possible view which declares that none of the others can stand alone and that if we cling to any one of them alone to the detriment of the others we merely limit the truth. This view is the philosophic. It declares that truth may be arrived at by combining all the other views which yield only partial truths into the balanced unity of whole truth, and unfolding the faculty of insight which penetrates into hidden reality.

I (PERSPECTIVES). 257

In the first stage of progress we learn to stand aside from the world and to still our thoughts about it. This is the mystical stage. Next, we recognize the world as being but a series of ideas within the mind; this is the mentalist-metaphysical stage. Finally, we return to the world's activity without reacting mentally to its suggestions, working disinterestedly, and knowing always that all is One. This is the philosophical stage.

XV.24.40

Although there are some points where they touch one another, there is a fundamental difference between philosophic detachment and the unassailable insensibility cultivated by the lower order of Hindu yogis or the invulnerable unfeelingness sought by the ancient Stoics. Some part of the philosopher remains an untouched, independent, and impartial observer. It notes the nature of things but does not allow itself to be swept away by the repulsiveness of unpleasant things or lost in the attractiveness of pleasant ones. But this does not prevent him from removing himself from the neighbourhood of the first kind, or from finding pleasure in the second kind. It is the same with his experience of persons. He is well aware of their characteristics; but however undesirable, faulty, or evil they may be, he makes no attempt to judge them. Indeed, he accepts them just as they are. This is inevitable since, being aware of his and their common origin in God, he practises goodwill towards everyone unremittingly.

XI.16.187

Just as convex and concave mirrors variously distort the images reflected in them, just as dirty, spotted, scratched, or cracked mirrors show a mixed, altered, or imperfect image of the object placed before them, so human minds variously distort or sully the spiritual truth revealed to them by the Overself. Rare is that one which lets the light shine forth unhindered, unchanged, and uncoloured. This is why the philosophic discipline, which exists for precisely such an objective, is so needed by every seeker after truth.

XI.16.313

Before he permits others to saddle him with the pretence of having achieved omniscience or to receive his pronouncements under the belief that he is incapable of making mistakes, the mystic needs to ask himself, 'What is the source of my revelation?' How far it may be trusted as being infallible depends on his discovery of the correct answer to this question, on his penetration through the relative elements in it to the absolute one, on his separation of the durable essence from the ephemeral covering.

XI.16.311

The ultimate unity of spiritual teachings, which some profess to see, applies rather to spiritual experience. As soon as the mystic attempts to understand, interpret, or communicate his experience, differences set in. This is partly because the intellect gets to work, partly because he unconsciously obeys the bias given him by the nature of his past experience, study, education, and environment, and partly because he may not have undergone the philosophic discipline to its fullest extent.

XI.16.9-10

Mysticism cannot continue to remain forever an esoteric system cultivated only by an exclusive coterie and unknown to the rest of humanity. It could easily remain aloof and apart only under the old forms of civilization, but not so easily under the new forms which are emerging today, with the immense widening of culture, communications, and privilege involved in them. We are indeed coming closer and closer to the time when more people shall be able to understand its teachings and many more people follow its techniques. The reasons which kept this knowledge hidden in the past, or in extremely limited circulation, are to a large extent less valid today. The spread of popular education helps to support this view, but there are other grounds. The fact is that esotericism has largely accomplished its function. So many conditions and circumstances which formerly justified its continuation have been so altered by time that they now justify not its cessation but, rather, its modification. The truth in its dazzling fullness could not be dispensed to the multitude while there was still no inward preparedness for its reception. If today the ban has been partially withdrawn, that is because there has been sufficient development to justify it. The old obscurantist attitude which would forbid public instruction in mysticism and prevent promiscuous circulation of mystical books cannot be fully justified today. The power which has been manifesting itself will sweep aside the resistance of such selfish exclusionists with the force of stunning shocks. If the esoteric path cannot entirely be made into a common highway, it can at least be made into a useful one for the increasing number of war-awakened minds who are fit to understand and follow it. Although the promiscuous communication of these teachings is still a rash and ill-advised undertaking, its judicious communication is now so no longer. If this integral philosophy can be interpreted to those few whose right knowledge and timely inspiration will thereby be used for the mental and physical betterment of the masses, it will surely be helping, however indirectly, the masses themselves. Taken as a whole, the masses are still not ready for the higher philosophy. But there are individuals as well as large groups among them who are quite ready for mysticism. It is a duty therefore to make it available to such individuals, to see that their inner needs are not neglected, and to leave all others to be taken care of by religion. The patriarchal age cannot last forever. Humanity is on the move. It is beginning to develop intellect, to read, learn, think and observe for itself. This is to some degree apparent everywhere, although its result will be apparent to the fullest degree only in a few. And these are the few who will accept and appreciate the philosophic mysticism here expounded. The others can be greatly helped by religious mysticism.

XIII.20.193–4

To view the inferior mystical experiences or the ratiocinative metaphysical findings otherwise than as passing phases, to set them up as finally representative of reality in the one case or of truth in the other, is to place them on a level to which they do not properly belong. Those who fall into the second error do so because they ascribe excessive importance to the thinking faculty. The mystic is too attached to one faculty, as the metaphysician is to the other, and neither can conduct a human being beyond the bounds of his enchained ego to the region where Being alone reigns. It is not that the mystic does not enter into contact with the Overself. He does. But his experience of the Overself is limited to glimpses which are partial, because he finds the Overself only within himself, not in the world outside. It is temporary because he has to take it when it comes at its own sweet will or when he can find it in meditation. It is a glimpse because it tells him about his own: 'I' but not about the 'Not-I'. On the other hand, the sage finds reality in the world without as his own self, at all times, and not at special occasions, and wholly rather than in glimpses. The mystic's light comes in glimpses, but the sage's is perennial. Whereas the first is like a flickering unsteady and uneven flame, the second is like a lamp that never goes out. Whereas the mystic comes into awareness of the Overself through feeling alone, the sage comes into it through knowledge plus feeling. Hence, the superiority of his realization.

The average mystic is devoid of sufficient critical sense. He delights in preventing his intellect from being active in such a definite direction. He has yet to learn that philosophical discipline has a steadying influence on the vagaries of mystical emotion, opinion, fancy, and experience. He refuses to judge the goal he has set up as to whether it be indeed man's ultimate goal. Consequently he is unable to apply correct standards whereby his own achievements or his own aspirations may be measured. Having shut himself up in a little heaven of his own, he does not attempt to distinguish it from other heavens or to discover if it be heaven indeed. He clings as stubbornly to his self-righteousness as does the religionist whom he criticizes for clinging to his dogma. He does not comprehend that he has transferred to himself that narrowness of outlook which he condemns in the materialistic. His position would be preposterous were it not so perilous.

Mysticism must not rest so smugly satisfied with its own obscurity that it refuses even to make the effort to come out into the light of critical self-examination, clear self-determination, and rational self-understanding. To complain helplessly that it cannot explain itself, to sit admiringly before its own self-proclaimed impalpability, or to stand aristocratically in the rarefied air of its own indefinability—as it usually does—is to fall into a kind of subtle quackery. Magnificent eulogy is no substitute for needed explanation.

XIII.20.202-3

The activity of analytic thinking has been banned in most mystical schools. They regard it as an obstacle to the attainment of spiritual consciousness. And ordinarily it is indeed so. For until the intellect can lie perfectly still, such consciousness cannot make itself apparent. The difficulty of making intellect quite passive is however an enormous one. Consequently different concentration techniques have been devised to overcome it. Nearly all of them involve the banishment of thinking and the cessation of reasoning. The philosophical school uses any or all of them where advisable but it also uses a technique peculiarly its own. It makes use of abstract concepts which are concerned with the nature of the mind itself and which are furnished by seers who have developed a deep insight into such nature. It permits the student to work out these concepts in a rational way but leading to subtler and subtler moods until they automatically vanish and thinking ceases as the transcendental state is induced to come of itself. This method is particularly suited either to those who have already got over the elementary difficulties of concentration or to those who regard reasoning power as an asset to be conserved rather than rejected. The conventional mystic, being the victim of external suggestion, will cling to the traditional view of his own school, which usually sees no good at all in reasoned thinking, and aver that spiritual attainment through such a path is psychologically impossible. Never having been instructed in it and never having tried it, he is not really in a position to judge.

XI.16.34

If a man gives up several hours every day to religious devotions, mystical exercises, and metaphysical study, but has not given up his feelings of envy, spite, and malice, then his spiritual development is a superficial affair. True spirituality always penetrates into a man's heart, changes his attitudes towards other people, and purifies his relations with them. If he has no results to show in the moral sphere, do not be deceived by his mystical tall talk or pious mouthings.

XIII.20.69

The faith in and the practice of reverential worship into which he was initiated by religion must not be dropped. It is required by philosophy also. Only, he is to correct, purify, and refine it. He is to worship the divine presence in his heart, not some distant remote being, and he is to do so more by an act of concentrated thought and unwavering feeling than by resort to external indirect and physical methods. With the philospher, as with the devotee, the habit of prayer is a daily one. But whereas he prays with light and heat, the other prays with heat alone. The heart finds in such worship a means of pouring out its deepest feelings of devotion, reverence, humility, and communion before its divine source. Thus we see that philosophy does not annul religious worship, but purifies and preserves what is best in it. It does annul the superstitions, exploitations, and futilities connected with conventional religious worship. In the end philosophy brings the seeker back to religion but not to *a* religion: to the reverence for a supreme power which he had discarded when he discarded the superstitions which had entwined themselves around it. Philosophy is naturally religious and inevitably mystical. Hence it keeps intact and does not break to pieces that which it receives from religion and yoga. It will, of course, receive only their sound fruits, not their bad ones. Philosophic endeavour does not, for instance, disdain religious worship and humble prayer merely because its higher elements transcend them. They are indeed part of such endeavour. But they are not, as with religionists, the whole of it. The mystic must not give up being religious merely because he has become a mystic. In the same way, the philosopher must not give up being both mystical and religious merely because he has become a philosopher. It is vitally important to know this. Philosophy does not supercede religion but keeps it and enlarges it.

XI.16.28

The devotional mystic enjoys being lifted up to rapturous heights. But insofar as he luxuriates in his mystical experience as he would luxuriate in a beautifully furnished bedroom, it is nothing more than a personal possession, a component of his private property. It is good that he has it, of course, but it is not enough. For how different is this from the philosophic experience, which opens egotistic ears to the call of mankind's needs! He will enjoy the thrills of being emotionally swept off his feet by mystical ecstasies: but when eventually he comes to understand, whether by his own intuition or by someone else's instruction, that such excitement prevents him from reaching the fullest consciousness of the Overself, he will come to respect the preachments of philosophy in this matter. Here an analogy may be useful to clarify our meaning. The mystic is like a man who carries away the flower, knowing that the perfume will come with it also. The mystic is so enraptured by the exalted ecstasy of peace of his experience that he tries to seize hold of it, only to find that it soon eludes his grasp. The philosopher does not dally his attention with the ecstasy of peace but directs it straight toward the source whence the peace emanates—to the Mind itself—and tries through comprehension to seize hold of its very nature. In the result he gets both reality and its emanated peace at the same time. He absorbs the ecstasy instead of being absorbed by it.

XII.18.75

The ordinary mystic who has surrendered his will to the Overself is like a man floating downstream in a boat with his eyes turned up to the sky and his hands folded in his lap. The philosophic mystic who has surrendered his will to the Divine is like a man floating downstream with his eyes gazing ahead, on the look-out, and his hands keeping firm hold of the rudder to steer the boat. The first man's boat may crash into another one or even into the riverbank at any moment. The second man's boat will safely and successfully navigate its way through these dangers. Yet both men are being supported and propelled by the same waters, both mystic and philosopher have given their self and life to the Divine. Nevertheless, the consequences are not and cannot be the same. For the first despises and refuses to use his God-given intelligence.

XI.16.64

The attainment of this deep state of oneness in meditation by an ordinary mystic may seem to be the end of the quest. Nevertheless the cycle of reincarnation will not end for him until he has become a philosophical mystic. For even though all earthly desires have been given a quietus, there will remain a latent desire to *know*, to understand his own experience and the world experience. To satisfy this desire, which will slowly come to the surface under the compulsion of Nature, he will have to develop intelligence to the proper degree. If he cannot do it quickly enough, then the work will have to continue into as many other births as are needed to finish it. For nature is shepherding the human race not only along the road of spiritual evolution but also of intellectual evolution.

XI.16.26

Buddha certainly glorified the worth of compassion, but he

also glorified the worth of insight. He never said that universal compassion could alone bring one to Nirvana. Buddha
recommended the first as a disciplinary practice for the
attainment of the other. Why? Because personal feeling either
blinds us to truth or distorts our mentality. Often we cannot see things as they really are because we are warped by
our egoistic prejudices and passions. Compassion thins the
ego's strength and assists us to become properly equipped
to achieve insight into Truth. Similarly, Jesus gave the masses
the golden rule of doing unto one's neighbour as one would
be done by. They needed to be dislodged from their strong
selfishness. Hence, he taught them that 'Whatsoever you sow
that shall you also reap' but he did not suggest that this was
sufficient guidance to the Kingdom of Heaven. Love is not
enough.

XIII.20.225-6

Such a revolutionary acquisition as insight must necessarily prove to be in a man's life can only be developed by over-
coming all the tremendous force of habitual wrong thinking,
by neutralizing all the tremendous weight of habitual wrong
feeling, and by counteracting all the tremendous strength
of habitual wrong-doing. In short, the familiar personal 'I'
must have the ground cut from under his feet. This is done
by the threefold discipline. The combined threefold technique consists of metaphysical reflection, mystical meditation, and constant remembrance in the midst of disinterested
active service. The full use and balanced exercise of every
function is needful. Although these three elements have here
been isolated one by one for the purpose of clearer intellectual study, it must be remembered that in actual life the student should not attempt to isolate them. Such a division is
an artificial one. He who takes for his province this whole
business of truth-seeking and gains this rounded all-
comprehensive view will no longer be so one-sided as to set
up a particular path as being the only way to salvation. On
the contrary, he will see that salvation is an integral matter.
It can no more be attained by mere meditation alone, for

example, than by mere impersonal activity alone; it can no more be reached by evading the lessons of everyday external living than by evading the suppression of such externality which meditation requires. Whereas metaphysics seeks to lift us up to the superphysical idea by thinking, whereas meditation seeks to lift us up by intuition, whereas ethics seeks to raise us to it by practical goodness, art seeks to do the same by feeling and appreciating beauty. Philosophy in its wonderful breadth and balance embraces and synthesizes all four and finally adds their coping stone, insight.

XIII.20.73–4

It is the joyous duty of philosophy to bring into systematic harmony the various views which mankind has held and will ever hold, however conflicting they seem on the surface, by assigning the different types to their proper levels and by providing a total view of the possible heights and depths of human thought. Thus and thus alone the most opposite tendencies of belief and the most striking contrasts of outlook are brought within a single scheme. All become aspects, more or less limited only. None ever achieves metaphysical finality and need ever again be mistaken for the whole truth. All becomes clear as organic phases of mankind's mental development. Philosophy alone can bring logically opposite doctrines into harmonious relation with each other by assigning them to their proper places under a single sheltering canopy. Thus out of the medley of voices within us philosophy creates a melody.

XI.16.67

The entry into objectless thought-free contemplation may be made year after year and a wonderful state it is too. But however pleasant and peaceful it is, the seeds of negative feelings are not made sterile but are only rendered inactive until new outer circumstances appear which bring them back to life—although the longer their suppression the weaker they become. Only knowledge of the truth and application of its understanding can end the bondage to ego where these tendencies lurk. Hence if the practice of contemplation is accompanied or followed or, although not usual, preceded by the path of knowledge, a real rooting-out of ego-bondage is possible. This alone leads to permanent reform of character and transformation of outlook. It is done by stages, or rather depths of insight, but the final one is quite abrupt.

XI.16.60

A common but wrong idea, into which some writers on mysticism fall, is that the final goal is realized by becoming one with the universe—a part of and united with Nature. That is indeed a state which often arises either on the way to the goal or on the return from it, but it is certainly not the ultimate goal itself. Man's highest source is in the infinite fullness of being whereas Nature is an expression of that being just as he is. It is the lesser thing, not the Ultimate Fact. The mystic's true goal must lie beyond it.

XIII.20.226

Philosophy must critically absorb the categories of metaphysics, mysticism, and practicality. For it understands that in the quest for truth the co-operation of all three will not only be helpful and profitable to each other but is also necessary to itself. For only after such absorption, only after it has travelled through them all can it attain what is beyond them all. The decisive point of this quest is reached after the co-operation between all three activities attains such a pitch that they become fused into a single all-comprehensive one which itself differs from them in character and qualities. For the whole truth which is then revealed is not merely a composite one. It not only absorbs them all but transcends them all. When water is born out of the union of oxygen and hydrogen, we may say neither that it is the same as the simple sum-total of both nor that it is entirely different from both. It possesses properties which they in themselves do not at all possess. We may only say that it includes and yet transcends them. When philosophic insight is born out of the union of intellectual reasoning, mystical feeling, and

altruistic doing, we may say neither that it is only the totali-
zation of these things nor that it is utterly remote from them.
It comprehends them all and yet itself extends far beyond
them into a higher order of being. It is not only that the
philosopher synthesizes these triple functions, that in one
and the same instant his intellect understands the world, his
heart feels a tender sympathy towards it, and his will is moved
to action for the triumph of good, but also that he is continuously conscious of that infinite reality which, in its purity,
no thinking, no emotion, and no action can ever touch.

XV.24.35-6

It is the business of philosophy to show us how to be nobly
serene. The aim is always to keep our thoughts as evenly
balanced in the mind as the Indian women keep the pitchers
of water which they may be carrying evenly balanced upon
their heads. A smugly self-satisfied, piously sleek com-
placency is not the sort of exalted serenity meant here. It
would indeed be fatal to true progress, and especially fatal
to the philosophic duty of making one's personal contribu-
tion toward the betterment of human existence. When such
equilibrium of mind is established, when the ups and downs
of external fortune are unable to disturb the inner balance
of feeling, reason, and intuition, and when the mechanical
reactions of the sense organs are effortlessly controlled, we
shall achieve a true, invincible self-sufficiency.

VIII.12.183

There are times—and they are the times when, looking back,
I love my profession most—when writing becomes for me
not a profession at all but either a form of religious worship
or a form of metaphysical enlightenment. It is then, as the
pen moves along silently, that I become aware of a shining
presence which calls forth all my holy reverence or pushes
open the mind's doors.

XIII.20.214

The philosopher is satisfied with a noble peace and does not

run after mystical ecstasies. Whereas other paths often
depend upon an emotionalism that perishes with the disap-
pearance of the primal momentum that inspired it, or which
dissolves with the dissolution of the first enthusiastic ecstasies themselves, here there is a deeper and more dependable
process. What must be emphasized is that most mystical
aspirants have an initial or occasional ecstasy, and they are
so stirred by the event that they naturally want to enjoy it
permanently. This is because they live under the common
error that a successful and perfect mystic is one who has
succeeded in stabilizing ecstasy. That the mystic is content
to rest on the level of feeling alone, without making his feeling self-reflective as well, partly accounts for such an error.
It also arises because of incompetent teachers or shallow
teaching, leading them to strive to perform what is imprac-
ticable and to yearn to attain what is impossible. Our warning is that this is not possible, and that however long a mystic
may enjoy these 'spiritual sweets', they will assuredly come
to an end one day. The stern logic of facts calls for stress
on this point. Too often he believes that this is the goal, and
that he has nothing more about which to trouble himself.
Indeed, he would regard any further exertions as a sacrile-
gious denial of the peace, as a degrading descent from the
exaltation of this divine union. He longs for nothing more
than the good fortune of being undisturbed by the world
and of being able to spend the rest of his life in solitary devotion to his inward ecstasy. For the philosophic mystic, however, this is not the terminus but only the starting point of
a further path. What philosophy says is that this is only a
preliminary mystical state, however remarkable and bliss-
ful it be. There is a more matured state—that of gnosis—
beyond it. If the student experiences paroxysms of ecstasy
at a certain stage of his inner course, he may enjoy them
for a time, but let him not look forward to enjoying them
for all time. The true goal lies beyond them, and he should
not forget that all-important fact. He will not find final salvation in the mystical experience of ecstasy, but he will find
an excellent and essential step towards salvation therein. He
who would regard rapturous mystical emotion as being the

same as absolute transcendental insight is mistaken. Such a mistake is pardonable. So abrupt and striking is the contrast with his ordinary state that he concludes that this condition of hyper-emotional bliss is the condition in which he is able to experience reality. He surrenders himself to the bliss, the emotional joy which he experiences, well satisfied that he has found God or his soul. But his excited feelings about reality are not the same as the serene experience of reality itself. This is what a mystic finds difficult to comprehend. Yet, until he does comprehend it, he will not make any genuine progress beyond this stage.

4

THE OVERSELF

XIV.22.92

We found it necessary, in the interests of greater precision and better exposition, to restrict the term 'Overself' to represent the ultimate reality of man, and to introduce the term 'World-Mind' to represent the ultimate reality of the universe.

XIV.22.93

There is some point in each individual being where the human and the divine must join, where man's little consciousness bends low before, or blends subtly with, the Universal Mind which is his ultimate source. It is impossible to describe that intersection in any terms which shall adequately fit it, but it can be named. In philosophy it is the Overself.

XIV.22.94

The Overself is the point where the One Mind is received into consciousness. It is the 'I' freed from narrowness, thoughts, flesh, passion, and emotion—that is, from the personal ego.

XIV.22.94

That point where man meets the Infinite is the Overself, where he, the finite, responds to what is absolute, ineffable and inexhaustible Being, where he reacts to That which transcends his own existence—this is the Personal God he experiences and comes into relation with. In this sense his belief in such a God is justifiable.

XIV.22.80

Nothing could be nearer to a man than the Overself for it is the source of his life, mind, and feeling. Nothing could be farther from him nevertheless, for it eludes all his familiar instruments of experience and awareness.

XIV.22.102

The mysterious character of the Overself inevitably puzzles the intellect. We may appreciate it better if we accept the paradoxical fact that it unites a duality and that therefore there are two ways of thinking of it, both correct. There is the divine being which is entirely above all temporal concerns, absolute and universal, and there is also the demi-divine being which is in historical relation with the human ego.

XIV.22.61

Although It is at the very heart of human beings, the Overself is very far from their present level of consciousness. Nothing could be closer yet this is the supreme paradox of our existence and the strangest enigma confronting our thought.

XIV.22.101

This is the paradox, that the Overself is at once universal and individual. It is the first because it overshadows all men as a single power. It is the second because it is found by each man within himself. It is both space and the point in space. It is infinite Spirit and yet it is also the holy presence in everyone's heart.

XIV.22.80

Although awareness is the first way in which we can regard

the soul or Overself, the latter is also that which makes awareness possible and hence a sub- or super-conscious thing. This explains why it is that we do not know our souls, but only our thoughts, our feelings, and our bodies. It is because we *are* the soul and hence we *are* the knower as well as the act of knowing. The eyes see everything outside yet do not see themselves.

XIV.22.102-3

Because of the paradoxically dual nature which the Overself possesses, it is very difficult to make clear the concept of the Overself. Human beings are rooted in the ultimate mind through the Overself, which therefore partakes on the one hand of a relationship with a vibratory world and on the other of an existence which is above all relations. A difficulty is probably due to the vagueness or confusion about which standpoint it is to be regarded from. If it is thought of as the human soul, then the vibratory movement is connected with it. If it is thought of as transcending the very notion of humanity, and therefore in its undifferentiated character, the vibratory movement must disappear.

XIV.22.103

If we are to think correctly, we cannot stop with thinking of the Overself as being only within us. After this idea has become firmly established for its metaphysical and devotional value, we must complete the concept by thinking of the Overself as being also without us. If in the first concept it occupies a point in space, in the second one it is beyond all considerations of place.

XIV.22.225

When the impeccable peace of the Overself inundates a man's heart, he finds that it is no negative thing. It must not be confused with the sinister calm of a graveyard or with the mocking immobility of a paralytic. It is a strong positive and enduring quality which is definitely enjoyable. We actually get a momentary and much-diluted sample of it at such times as when a hated object is *suddenly* removed from our path, when a powerful ancient ambition is *suddenly* realized, or when we meet a greatly beloved person after long absence. Why? Because at such moments we are freed from the infatuation with the hatred, the ambition, or the love, simply because they have achieved their object and the desire-thoughts become still. The freedom passes almost in a flash, however, because some other infatuation replaces it in the heart within a few moments and thoughts begin their movement again.

XIV.22.103

We may take comfort in the fact that the Overself never at any moment abandons or obliterates the human personality, however debased it becomes. Nor could it do so, whatever foolish cults say to the contrary, for through this medium it finds an expression in time-space.

XIV.22.103

When we say the Overself is within the heart, it would be a great error to think that we mean it is limited to the heart. For the heart is also within it. This seeming paradox will yield to reflection and intuition. The mysterious relationship between the ego and the Overself has been expressed by Jesus in the following words: 'The Father is in the Son, and the Son is in the Father.'

XIV.22.80

This is the abiding essence of a man, his true self as against his ephemeral person. Whoever enters into its consciousness enters into timelessness, a wonderful experience where the flux of pleasures and pains comes to an end in utter serenity, where regrets for the past, impatience at the present, and fears of the future are unknown.

XIV.22.103

The dictionary defines *individuality* as separate and distinct existence. Both the ego and the Overself have such an existence. But whereas the ego has this and nothing more, the Overself has this consciousness within the universal existence. That is why we have called it the *higher individuality*.

XI.16.298

The Overself can never be seen or heard, touched or tasted. Therefore no visions of a pictorial kind, no voices of a psychic kind, no musical sounds of a 'mystical and cosmic' kind, no outer form of manifestation of any kind which comes to you through the senses can be the real authentic experience of it.

XV.24.89

It is nice and noble to talk about becoming an instrument in God's hands, a channel of the Overself. But this is still an inferior relationship. It is not the highest kind. It is still occupied with the ego. Ascend to a higher level, give yourself completely to, and talk about, the higher power alone.

XIV.22.82

Let no one imagine that contact with the Overself is a kind of dreamy reverie or pleasant, fanciful state. It is a vital relationship with a current of peace, power, and goodwill flowing endlessly from the invisible centre to the visible self.

XV.23.187-8

If we search into the innermost part of our self, we come in the end to an utter void where nothing from the outside world can reflect itself, to a divine stillness where no image and no form can be active. This is the essence of our being. This is the true Spirit.

XIV.22.96

Although the Overself does not pass through the diverse experiences of its imperfect image, the ego, nevertheless it witnesses them. Although it is aware of the pain and pleasure experienced by the body which it is animating, it does not itself feel them; although detached from physical sensations, it is not ignorant of them. On the other hand, the personal consciousness does feel them because it regards them as states of its own self. Thus the Overself is conscious of our joys and sorrows without itself sharing them. It is aware of our sense-experience without itself being physically sentient. Those who wonder how this is possible should reflect that a man awakened from a nightmare is aware once again in the form of a revived memory of what he suffered and what he sensed but yet does not share again either the suffering or the sensations.

XIV.22.72-3

There is much confusion of understanding about what happens to the ego when it attains the ultimate goal. Some believe that a cosmic consciousness develops, with an all-knowing intelligence and an 'all-overish' feeling. They regard it as unity with the whole universe. Others assert that there is a complete loss of the ego, an utter destruction of the personal self. No—these are confused notions of what actually occurs. The Overself is not a collective entity as though it were composed of a number of particles. One's embrace of other human beings through it is not in union with them but only in sympathy, not in psychic identification with them but in psychic harmony. He has enlarged the area of his vision and sees himself as a part of mankind. But this does not mean that he has become conscious of all mankind as though they were himself. The true unity is with one's own higher indestructible self. It is still with a higher individuality, not a cosmic one, and it is still with one's own self, not with the rest of mankind. Unity with them is neither mystically nor practically possible. What we discover is discovered by a deepening of consciousness, not by a widening of it. Hence it is not so much a wider as a deeper self that he has first to find.

With the rectification of this error, we may find the correct answer to the question: 'What is the practical meaning of the injunction laid by all the great spiritual teachers upon their followers, to give up the ego, to renounce the self?' It does not ask for a foolish sentimentality, in the sense that we are to be as putty in the hands of all other men. It does not ask for an utter impossibility, in the sense that we are never to attend to our own affairs at all. It does not ask for a useless absurdity, in the sense that we are to become oblivious of our very existence. On the contrary, it asks for what is wise, practicable, and worthwhile—that we give up our lower personality to our higher individuality.

Thus it is not that the aspirant is asked to abandon all thought of his particular self (as if he could) or to lose consciousness of it, but that he is asked to perceive its imperfection, its unsatisfactoriness, its faultiness, its baseness and its sinfulness and, in consequence of this perception, to give it up in favour of his higher self, with its perception, blessedness, goodness, nobility, and wisdom. For in the lower ego he will never know peace whereas in the diviner one he will always know it.

XVI.26.91-4

What is the use, ask many questioners, of first, an evolution of the human soul which merely brings it back to the same point where it started and second, of developing a selfhood through the long cycles of evolution only to have it merged or dissolved in the end into the unselfed Absolute? Is not the whole scheme absurdly useless? The answer is that if this were really the case, the criticism passed would be quite a fair one. But it is not the case. The unit of life emanated from the Overself begins with the merest glimmer of consciousness, appearing on our plane as a protozoic cell. It evolves eventually into the fullest human consciousness, including the intellectual and spiritual. It does not finish as it began; on the contrary, there is a grand purpose behind all its travail. There is thus a wide gulf between its original state and its final one. The second point is more difficult to clear up, but it may be plainly affirmed that man's individuality survives even in the divinest state accessible to him. There it becomes the same in quality but not identical in essence. The most intimate mental and physical experiences of human love cast a little light for our comprehension of this mystery. The misunderstanding which leads to these questions arises chiefly because of the error which believes that it is the divine soul which goes through all this pilgrimage by reincarnating in a series of earthly forms. The true teaching about reincarnation is not that the divine soul enters into the captivity and ignorance of the flesh again and again, but that something emanated from the soul, that is, a unit of life that eventually develops into the personal ego, does so. The Overself contains this reincarnating ego within itself but does not itself reincarnate. It is the parent; the ego is only its offspring. The long and tremendous evolution through which the unit of life passes from its primitive cellular existence to its matured human one is a genuine evolution of its consciousness. Whoever believes that the process first plunges a soul down from the heights into a body or forces Spirit to lose itself in Matter, and then leaves it no alternative but to climb all the way back to the lost summit again, believes wrongly. The Overself never descends or climbs, never loses its own sublime consciousness. What really does this is something that emanates from it and that consequently holds its capacity and power in latency, something which is finited out of the Overself's infinitude and becomes first, the simple unit of life and later, the complex human ego. It is not the Overself that suffers and struggles during this long unfoldment but its child, the ego. It is not the Overself that slowly expands its intelligence and consciousness, but the ego. It is not the Overself that gets deluded by ignorance and passion, by selfishness and extroversion, but the ego.

The belief in the merger of the ego held by some Hindu sects or in its annihilation held by some Buddhists ones, is unphilosophical. The 'I' differentiated itself out of the infinite ocean of Mind into a distinct individuality after a long development through the diverse kingdoms of Nature. Having thus arrived at consciousness of what it is, having travelled the spiral of growth from germ to man, the result of all this effort is certainly not gained only to be thrown away.

Were this to happen then the entire history of the human race would be a meaningless one, its entire travail a resultless one, its entire aspiration a valueless one. If evolution were merely the complementary return journey of an involutionary process, if the evolving entity arrived only at its starting point for all its pains, then the whole plan would be a senseless one. If the journey of man consisted of nothing more than treading a circle from the time of his emergence from the Divine Essence to the time of his mergence back into it, it would be a vain and useless activity. It would be a stupendous adventure but also a stupid one. There is something more than that in his movement. Except in the speculations of certain theorists, it simply does not happen.

The self-consciousness thus developed will not be dissolved, extinguished, or re-absorbed into the Whole again, leaving not a trace behind. Rather will it begin a new spiral of evolution towards higher altitudes of consciousness and diviner levels of being, in which it will co-operate as harmoniously with the universal existence as formerly it collided against it. It will not separate its own good from the general good. Here is a part of the answer to this question: What are the ultimate reasons for human wanderings through the world-process? That life matters, that the universe possesses meaning, and that the evolutionary agonies are leading to something worthwhile—these are beliefs we are entitled to hold. If the cosmos is a wheel which turns and turns endlessly, it does not turn aimlessly. Evolution does not return us to the starting point as we were. The ascent is not a circle but a spiral.

Evolution presupposes that its own possibility has always been latent within the evolving entities. Hence the highest form is hidden away in the lowest one. There is development from the blindly instinctive life of animals to the consciously thinking life of man. The blind instinctive struggles of the plant to sustain itself are displaced in the evolutionary process by the intelligent self-conscious efforts of the man. Nor does this ascent end in the Vedantic merger or the Buddhistic annihilation. It could not, for it is a development of the individuality. Everywhere we find that evolution produces variety. There are myriads of individual entities, but each possesses some quality of uniqueness which distinguishes it from all others. Life may be one but its multitudinous expressions do differ, as though difference were inherent in such expression.

Evolution as mentalistically defined by philosophy is not quite the same as evolution as materialistically defined by Darwin. With us it is simply the mode of striving, through rhythmic rise and fall, for an ever fuller expansion of the individual unit's consciousness. However, the ego already possesses all such possibilities latently. Consequently the whole process, although apparently an ascending one, is really an unfolding one.

(Dated April 1963)

5

GRACE AND THE SHORT PATH

XII.18.113

When the ego is sufficiently crushed by its frustrations or failures—and sooner or later this may happen to most of us—it will turn, either openly or secretly, to the admission that it needs outside help. And what other help can it then find than Grace, whether mediated directly from the Overself or indirectly through a master?

XII.18.99

I know that many dispute the existence of Grace, especially those who are Buddhistically minded, strictly rational, and they have much ground for their stand. My own knowledge may be illusory, but my experience is not; from both knowledge and experience I must assert that through one channel or another Grace may come: dutiful, compassionate, and magnanimous.

XII.18.106-7

There are three types of Grace: firstly, that which has the appearance of Grace but which actually descends out of past good karma and is entirely self-earned; secondly, that which a Master gives to disciples or aspirants when the proper external and internal circumstances exist—this is in the nature of a temporary glimpse only but is useful because it gives a glimpse of the goal, a sense of the right direction, and inspiring encouragement to continue on the Quest; thirdly, when a man attains the fullest degree of realization, he is enabled in some cases to modify overhanging negative karma or in others to negate it because he has mastered the particular lessons that needed to be learned. This is particularly evident when the Hand of God removes obstructions in the path of his work. The philosophic conception of Grace shows it to be just and reasonable. It is indeed quite different from the orthodox religious belief about it, a belief which regards it as an arbitrary intervention by the Higher Power for the benefit of its human favourites.

XII.18.136

If a man misses the chance when grace is offered him interally by impersonal leadings or externally by a personal master, he will have to wait several years before the possibility of its recurrence can arise, if it does arise at all. In the same form, unobstructed by the disadvantages accumulated during the years, it can never arise again. Therefore it behoves him to be heedful that spiritual opportunity does not pass him by unrecognized or unseized. In this affair, the heart is often a better guide than the head, for the intellect doubts and wavers where intuition inclines and impels.

XII.18.102

Grace is not necessarily bestowed deliberately or conferred personally. It may be received from someone who does not even know that he is its source. It may manifest through nothing more than the physical meeting between these two, or through a letter from one to the other, or even through the mere thinking about one of them by the other person. But, however obtained, Grace has its ultimate source in the mysterious Overself. This is why no man, however saintly, exalted, or advanced, can really give it to anyone: he can only be used by the higher power for this purpose, whether aware or unaware in the surface part of his mind of what is happening.

XII.18.104

No man has the right or capacity to dispense grace, but some

men may sometimes be used by the higher power in effect-
ing its own dispensations.

XII.18.104

It was not Christ's death that brought his grace into the
human world, but his life.

XII.18.102

He may receive grace directly from its source in the infinite
love, power, and wisdom of the Overself, or indirectly
through personal contact with some inspired man, or still
more indirectly through such a man's intellectual or artistic
productions.

XII.18.102-3

The philosophic concept of Grace is different from, and not
to be confounded with, the popular religio-theologic one.
The latter carries arbitrariness, caprice, and favouritism
within it. The former has nothing of the kind. Despite its
mysteriousness, it often follows the fulfilment of certain conditions by the seeker, but even when it does not appear to
do so, it is a legacy from causes set going in earlier lives on
this earth. The notion that it is dispensed in an arbitrary manner by the Higher Power is to anthropomorphize that Power,
to regard it as a glorified man. This is nonsense to anyone
who can reflect correctly and think deeply on the Power's
real nature. The notion of caprice is to make the manifestation of Grace an affair of mere whimsy, an emotion of the
moment, a passing mood. This simply could not be, for grace
descends from a plane which transcends such things. Lastly,
the notion of favouritism is usually applied in connection
with a guru, a holy man, or a godlike man. If such a man
is really, fully, and profoundly illumined, he has goodwill
to all other people, wishes that all shall come to the Light,
not just those he favours or who favour him. His grace is
always there, but men must be able to recognize him and
accept it. He is *always* ready to share his experience of the
divine ever-presence with everyone, but not everyone is

ready to receive it. In short, grace is what comes to you from an inspired book, or a blessed letter, or a few moments of relaxation.

XV.23.143

Scott in his search for the South Pole amid ice-bound Antarctic wastes and Smythe in his quest for the summit of Mount Everest amid terrible avalanches of stone and snow, reported in their written accounts the sense of not being alone, of being companioned by a mystic unseen presence which bestowed a strange calm. Scott's venture ended in heroic death whereas Smythe survived to enjoy the warmth and safety of his home. Both however knew what it was to be uncommonly blessed at the time, for Scott passed to his fated death with an utter serenity and an inward trust in its aftermath which took all the horror out of it for him. This noble passage to another stage of existence was not the miserable calamity which it was for many other men. What was the mystic presence which walked beside these men? Each may have had his own belief about it, may have constructed in imagination what his previous knowledge, experience, tendencies and outlook may have naturally persuaded him to construct. Each therefore may have had different ideas about it, but this would not affect the actual power which inspired and animated him at the time. For that power was nothing less than the Grace of the Overself, and if we understand the psychological secret of what happened to Scott and Smythe we may then understand that it is not only far-wandering explorers and high-climbing mountaineers who may call up the Overself by their brave trust. The same dangerous experience which has brought fear, horror, and despair to other men brought them dignified confidence and mystical enlargement of consciousness which made them aware for the time of the hidden observer. They had indeed suddenly but partially stepped into the transcendental state. Whoever successfully practises the Hidden Observer meditation will experience precisely the same sense of not being alone, of being companioned by a mystic presence which brings with it a benign sense of assurance and security. He will, however, experience much more than that.

XII.18.140

That enlightenment is a transfiguring event which not only revolutionizes general outlook but also changes moral character, there is testimony enough for anyone in the archives of mystical biography. The old self is laid aside as too imperfect, the old weaknesses are drowned in the overwhelming tide of Grace which pours through the man and his life.

XV.23.4

This then is the ultimate truth—that in our inmost nature we are anchored in God, inseparable from God, and that the discovery of this heavenly nature is life's loftiest purpose. Even now, already, today, we are as divine as we ever shall be. The long evolutionary ladder which by prophets and teachers, gurus, and guides we are bidden to climb toilsomely and slowly and painfully need not be climbed at all if only we heed this truth continually, if we refuse to let it go, if we make it ours in all parts of our being—in thought, feeling, faith, and action.

XV.23.3

Consciousness appearing as the person seeks itself. This is its quest. But when it learns and comprehends that it is itself the object of that quest, the person stops not only seeking outside himself but even engaging in the quest itself. Henceforth he lets himself be moved by the Overself's flow.

XV.23.14

He sees the truth as with a jolt. There it is, within his own being, lying deep down but still in his own self. There never was any need to travel anywhere to find it; no need to visit anyone who was supposed to have it already, and sit at his feet; not even to read any book, however sacred or inspired.

Nor could another person, place, or writing give it to him—
he would have to unveil it for himself in himself. The others,
could direct him to look inwards, thus saving all the effort
of looking elsewhere. But he himself would have to give the
needful attention to himself. The discovery must be his own,
made within the still centre of his being.

XV.23.118

Ramana Maharshi was quite right. Pruning the ego of some
faults will only be followed by the appearance and growth
of new faults! Of what use is it so long as the ego remains
alive? Hence the failure of mankind's moral history to show
any real progress over the past three thousand years, despite
the work of Buddha, Jesus, and other Messiahs. The correct course, which has always been valid for the individual,
is just as valid for all mankind—get at the root, the source,
the ego itself. But although Maharshi was right, his teaching gives only part of Truth's picture. Presented by itself, and
without the other part, it is not only incomplete but may
even become misleading. By itself it seems to indicate that
there is no need to work on our specific weaknesses, that
they can be left untouched while we concentrate on the
essential thing—rooting out the ego. But where are the
seekers who can straightaway and successfully root it out?
For the very strength of purpose and power of concentration needed for this uprooting will be sapped by their faults.

XV.23.10-11

All pruning of the ego is of little use, for as one fault is
removed a new one springs out of latency. Why? Because
the ego *is*. The Short Path is the only genuine approach to
truth, the only one offering real possibility of liberation. It
is endorsed by Atmananda and Krishnamurti and Ramana
Maharshi. Lifetimes have been spent by seekers who have
travelled the Long Path but arrived nowhere, or are not much
nearer the goal, whereas others have made swift advance
from their first steps on the Short Path. The assertion that
the Long Path is a necessary complement to or preparation

for the Short one is correct only for those who are still under the thraldom of illusion, who are asleep. Its followers merely travel in a circle: they never get out of the illusion or awake from the sleep. That is why in the end it has to be given up, abandoned, understood for the egoistic effort that it really is. The entire length of the Long Path is an attempt at self-improvement and self-purification planned, managed, operated, and supervised by the ego itself. Is it conceivable that the ego will work for its own destruction? No!—it will never do that however much it pretends to do so, however subtle the bluff with which it deceives itself or others. Even when the ego rebels against itself, it is merely playing a part. It has played many different parts in the past. Appearing as a rebel is merely one more disguise in the whole series.

XV.23.40-1

The truth of Zen attitude—letting go of restraints, avoiding reflection, refraining from self-observation, acting spontaneously, and being natural—is that it is true only on the intuitive level. It is there the only proper and possible attitude. But how few have really attained this level! How many have merely taken their very ordinary impulses, their very human desires, their very animal lusts, for profound intuitions! Thus they merely continue to act as they would have acted anyway, for the same reasons and by the same motives. The results will continue to be the same too. They are as far from true enlightenment as everyone else but with this great difference: that whereas the others do not pretend to be superior or illumined, they do. It is a fantastic self-deception, a foolish egoism that if exaggerated could lead to lunacy. Only a master can hold such an attitude with perfect fitness and propriety, only such a one can afford to 'let go' of all self-control without falling into the dangerous swirling waters which are always ready to engulf the man who behaves as he pleases, and gives himself up with complete abandon to what he wrongly imagines is 'walking on'. This is why the earlier Chinese Zen lectures and writings were often prefaced by the warning that they were intended for persons who were already properly instructed *and established* in 'the virtues'. Therefore the modern Western beginners should not let the temptation to exploit Zen for their own personal purposes lead them into a trap. The only 'letting go' that they can safely indulge in is to let go of the ego, the only safe 'walking on' is to walk away from their attachments.

XV.23.37

Those who believe in the Short Path of sudden attainment, such as the sectarian following of Ramana Maharshi and the koan-puzzled intellectuals of Zen Buddhism, confuse the first flash of insight which unsettles everything so gloriously with the last flash which settles everything even more gloriously. The disciple who wants something for nothing, who hopes to get to the goal without being kept busy with arduous travels to the very end, will not get it. He has to move from one point of view to a higher, from many a struggle with weaknesses to their mastery. Then only, when he has done by himself what he should do, may he cease his efforts, be still, and await the influx of Grace. Then comes light and the second birth.

XV.23.188

That which IS, by its very nature, is out of time—while thinking involves a series of points in time. Thinking is finite and limits awareness to finite objects. Therefore, to contact the *infinite* we must go beyond thought. Because human intellect is too finite, it follows that our thoughts cannot encompass it. Since that which IS cannot be taken hold of by thinking of any kind, a part of the essential requirement for contact with it is the non-acting of the thinking function. The mind must be emptied of all its contents in order that its true nature—awareness—should be revealed. At present, it is always entangled with some thoughts so that awareness by itself is lost in that thought. Self disappears in the ego-thought, and the 'I' mistakes the object for the sub-

ject—whether the object be the world outside it, or thoughts
inside it.

XIII.19.88

Present time never stands still, it is always moving away. That
is one reason why we are enjoined to '*Be still*' if we would
know we are like God at base. In the mind's deep stillness
we live neither in past memories nor future fears and hopes,
nor in the moving present, but only in an emptiness which
is the everlasting Now. Here alone we can remain in
unbroken peace, paid for by being devoid of expectations
and free from desires, cut off from attachments and above
the day's agitations or oscillations.

XV.23.224-5

Whoever succeeds in going down deeply enough into his
own consciousness can find a phase where it passes away
as person, as the limited little self, but is transformed into the
Universal being and then, still farther, into the Void. This
Void is not the annihilation of Consciousness but the fullness of it, not blankness but true awareness, unhindered by
subsiding activities, not the adulteration of it by thoughts
or imaginations but the purity of it. In this way he experiences his own personal self-nothingness. From this he
can understand two things: why so many prophets have
taught that self blocks our way and why the Mahayana
Buddhists have taught the reality of the Void.

XV.23.205

There, in the deepest state of contemplation, the awareness
of a second thing—whether this be the world of objects outside or the world of thoughts inside—vanishes. *But unconsciousness does not follow.* What is left over is a continuous static
impersonal and unchanging consciousness. This is the inmost
being of man. This is the supreme Self, dwelling within itself
alone. Its stillness transcends the activity of thinking, of the
knowing which distinguishes one thing from another. It is
incommunicable then, inexplicable later. But after a while

from this high level the meditator must descend, returning to his human condition. He has come as close in the contact with the Great Being, the most refined ultimate Godhead, as is possible. Let him be grateful. Let him not ask for more for *he* cannot know or experience more. This is as far as any man can go, for 'Thou shalt not see God and live.'

XV.23.224

When he travels the course of meditation into the deep places of his being, and if he plumbs them to their utmost reach, at the end he crosses the threshold of the Void and enters a state which is nonbeing to the ego. For no memory and no activity of his personal self can exist there. Yet it is not annihilation, for one thing remains—Consciousness. In this way, and regarding what happens from the standpoint of his ordinary state at a later time, he learns that this residue is his real being, his very Spirit, his enduring life. He learns too why every moment which takes him out of the Void stillness into a personal mental activity is a return to an inferior state and a descent to a lower plane. He sees that among such movements there must necessarily be classed even the answering of such thoughts as 'I am a Master. He is my disciple,' or 'I am being used to heal the disease of this man.' In his own mind he is neither a teacher nor a healer. If other men choose to consider him as such and gain help toward sinlessness or get cured of sickness, he takes no credit to himself for the result but looks at it as if the 'miracle' were done by a stranger.

XV.23.222

Those who find that beyond the Light they must pass through the Void, the unbounded emptiness, often draw back affrighted and refuse to venture farther. For here they have naught to gain or get, no glorious spiritual rapture to add to their memories, no great power to increase their sense of being a co-worker with God. Here their very life-blood is to be squeezed out as the price of entry; here they must become the feeblest of creatures.

XV.23.220

Students draw back affrighted at the concept of a great void which leaves them nothing, human or divine, to which they may cling. How much the more will they draw back, not from a mere concept, but from an actual experience through which they must personally pass! Yet this is an event, albeit not the final one on the ultimate ultramystic path, which they can neither avoid or evade. It is a trial which must be endured, although to the student who has resigned himself to acceptance of the truth whatever face it bears—who has consequently comprehended already the intellectual emptiness of both Matter and Personality—this experience will not assume the form of a trial but rather of an adventure. After such a rare realization, he will emerge a different man. Henceforth he will know that nothing that has shape, nobody who bears a form, no voice save that which is soundless can ever help him again. He will know that his whole trust, his whole hope, and his whole heart are now and forevermore to be surrendered unconditionally to this Void which mysteriously will no longer be a Void for him. For it is God.

XV.23.231

A further result of this contemplation of the world as the great Void is that the work done by mentalistic study is advanced still further, for not only are the things experienced by the five senses seen to be only thoughts but the thoughts themselves are now seen to be the transient spume and spray flung out of seeming Emptiness. Thus there is a complete reorientation from thoughts to Thought. Instead of holding a single thought or scenes of ideas in perfect concentration, the practiser must now move away from all ideas altogether to that seeming emptiness in which they arise. And the latter, of course, is the pure, passive, undifferentiated mind-stuff out of which the separate ideas are produced. Here there is no knowing and discriminating between one idea and another, no stirring into consciousness of this and that, but rather a sublime vacancy. For the Mind-essence is not something which we can picture to ourselves; it is utterly formless. It is as empty and as ungraspable as space.

XV.23.244

As I gaze upon the rigid, rapt figure of the Buddha upon my desk, I realize anew how much of Gautama's power is drawn from the practice of contemplation. It ties wings to the mind and sends the soul soaring up to its primal home. Gautama found his peace during that wonderful night when he came, weary of long search, dejected with six years of fruitless effort, to the Bo-tree near Gaya and sat in motionless meditation beneath its friendly branches, sinking the plummet of mind into the sacred well within. The true nature of human existence is obscured by the ceaseless changes of human thought. While we remain embroiled in the multitude of thoughts which pass and re-pass, we cannot discover the pure unit of consciousness which exists beneath them all. These thoughts must first be steadied, next stilled. Every man has a fount within him. He has but to arise and go unto it. There he may find what he really needs.

XV.23.244

The traditional Buddhist belief that all happiness must in the end change into unhappiness is not a cheerful one. It need never be taken too literally as being universally true, nor by itself alone, for there are counter-weighting truths. When Buddha brought to an end the meditation which culminated in final enlightenment, dawn was just breaking.

The last star which vanished with the night and the first one which he saw as he raised his head was Venus. What was his inner state, then? Did it synchronize with the reputed planetary influence of Venus—joyous and happy felicity—or with the gloomy view of life which tradition later associated with Buddhism? Who that has had a glimpse of those higher states, felt their serenity, can doubt it was the first? The Overself is not subjected to suffering. But this is not to say that it is bubbling with happiness. It is rather like an immensely deep ocean, perfectly tranquil below the surface.

That tranquillity is its ever-present condition and is a true joyousness which ordinary people rarely know. This is what Buddha felt. This is what he called NIRVANA.

6

WORLD-MIND AND MIND

XVI.25.3

We see plenty of evidence that the universe is not mindless, and therefore that there is a Universal Mind related to it—that is to say, related to us, who are parts of the whole.

XII.18.10

That which I address as 'O Mind of the World!' and whom Kabbalists address as 'Master of the Worlds!'—That which is without name or face or form, That alone I worship. That upon which all things depend but itself depends on nothing. That I revere. That which is unseen by all beings but which itself sees all, That I worship.

XVI.26.10

Whatever we call it, most people feel—whether vaguely or strongly—that there must be a God and that there must be something which God has in view in letting the universe come into existence. This purpose I call the World-Idea, because to me God is the World's Mind. This is a thrilling conception. It was an ancient revelation which came to the first cultures, the first civilizations, of any importance, as it has come to all others which have appeared, and it is still coming today to our own. With this knowledge, deeply absorbed and properly applied, man comes into harmonious alignment with his Source.

XVI.26.28–9

It is not only man that is made in the image of God: the whole universe is also an image of God. It is not only by coming to know himself that man discovers the divine life hidden deep in his heart: it is also by listening in the stillness of Nature to what she is forever declaring, that he discovers the presence of an infinite World-Mind.

XVI.26.12

When the revelation of the World-Idea came to religious mystics they could only call it 'God's Will'. When it came to the Greeks they called it 'Necessity'. The Indians called it 'Karma'. When its echoes were heard by scientific thinkers they called it 'the laws of Nature'.

XVI.27.15

The World-Mind brings our universe into being and governs it, too. The enormous number of objects and creatures which appear through Its agency, through Its power and wisdom, cannot be limited to what is visible alone, and must fill a thinking person with wonder at all the possibilities—a wonder which Plato said must be the beginning of philosophy.

XVI.26.11

The World-Idea holds within itself the laws which rule the world, the supreme intention which dominates it, and the invisible pattern which forms it.

XVI.26.11

There is an infinite number of possibilities in the evolution of man and the universe. If only certain ones out of them are actually realized, this is because both follow a pattern—the World-Idea.

XVI.26.11

The World-Idea provides secret invisible patterns for all

things that have come into existence. These are not necessarily the forms that our limited perceptions present to us but the forms that are ultimate in God's Will.

XVI.26.15

The World-Idea must not be regarded as something inert, nor only as a pattern, but also as a force through which the World-Mind acts, and through which it moves the universe.

XVI.26.15

The World-Idea would be more correctly understood for what it is if regarded as something dynamic and not static. It is a mental wave, forever flowing, rather than a rigid pattern.

XVI.26.11

Just as the World-Idea is both the expression of the World-Mind and one with it, so the *Word* (*Logos*) mentioned in the New Testament as being with God is another way of saying the same thing. The world with its form and history is the embodiment of the *Word* and the *Word* is the World-Idea.

XVI.26.15

It is a paradox of the World-Idea that it is at once a rigid pattern and, within that pattern, a latent source of indeterminate possibilities. This seems impossible to human minds, but it would not be the soul of a divine order if it were merely mechanical.

XVI.26.69–70

Revelation establishes that the sequence of events in our universe is an orderly one, while observation confirms it. They do not just happen by chance, and chaos is not their background. Many will admit this but yet they are unable to admit that this orderliness is not limited to stars and planets alone, nor to the chemical elements also, nor to the physical forces of Nature in addition. They are unable to extend

it to human life, to its birth, course, fortunes, and death. But
the philosophic revelation tells us that law and order are here
not less than elsewhere. It is unreasonable to suggest that
although they rule all the lower kingdoms, they do not touch
us. Our experiences too are controlled by heaven's laws.

XVI.27.20

The point which appears in space is a point of light. It spreads
and spreads and spreads and becomes the World-Mind. God
has emerged out of Godhead. And out of the World-Mind
the world itself emerges—not all at once, but in various
stages. From that great light come all other and lesser lights,
come the suns and the planets, the galaxies, the universes,
and all the mighty hosts of creatures small and great, of
beings just beginning to sense and others fully conscious,
aware, wise. And with the world appear the opposites, the
dual principle which can be detected everywhere in Nature,
the yin and yang of Chinese thought.

XVI.26.41

The World-Mind is able to think the World-Idea only under
the form of opposite conditions existing at the same time.
No world could possibly come into existence without these
contrasts and differences. The presence accounts for the existence of the universe; their movement toward equilibrium
with one another accounts for its history.

XVI.26.43

We could see no form of anything at all if all were in the
dark nor even if all were in the light. The contrast of shadow
and light is needed to define the form. Opposites are always
necessary to each other. This is why they are present
throughout the universe and moreover present in all possible combinations and proportions in all possible rhythms
and patterns. It is present in life, in all things, in planets and
seasons. It is the eternal and invariable law of manifested
existence.

XVI.26.48

Experience teaches human beings that life is governed by
duality, that like Nature itself, it holds contrasts and oppositions within itself. Just as day and night are positive and
negative poles, so are joy and sorrow. But just as there is a
point where day meets night, a point which we call the
twilight, so in our experience, human experience, the joys
and sorrows have a neutral point—and in Nature, an equilibrium. So the mind must find its own equilibrium, and thus
it will find its own sense of peace. To see that duality governs
everything is to see why human life is one tremendous
paradox.

XVI.26.45

It would be a mistake to believe that these two forces,
although so very different from each other, are fighting each
other. This is not so. They are to be regarded as complementary to one another. They are like positive and negative poles
in electricity, and they must exist together or die together.
They are inseparable, but the need between them is correct
balance, or equilibrium.

XVI.26.56

Why should the waves of life-entities take this spiral-like two-
way course? Why do they not go along a direct single one?
The answer is that they have to gather experience to grow;
if this experience includes totally opposed conditions, *all* the
parts of each entity can grow, all its latent qualities can be
stirred into unfoldment. In the oppositions of birth and death,
growth and decay, in-breathing and exhaling, youth and age,
joy and suffering, introversion and extroversion, spirit-form
and body-form, it fulfils itself.

XVI.27.17

Were the World-Mind beyond, because outside, the finite
universe, then it would be limited by that universe and thus
lose its own infinitude. But because *it includes* the universe

completely within itself while remaining completely
unlimited, it is genuinely infinite. World-Mind is neither
limited nor dissipated by its self-projection in the universe.
If World-Mind is immanent in the universe, it is not confined to the universe; if it is present in every particle of the
All, its expression is not exhausted by the All.

XV1.26.24

The cosmos is neither a phantom to be disdained nor an illusion to be dismissed. It is a remote expression in time and
space and individuality of that which is timeless, spaceless
and infinite. If it is not the Reality in its ultimate sense, it
is an emanation of the Reality. Hence it shares in some way
the life of its source. To find that point of sharing is the true
object of incarnation for all creatures within the cosmos.

XVI.26.70

You are part of the World-Mind's World-Idea. Therefore, you
are a part of its purpose too. Seek to be shown what that
is, and how you may realize it, rather than mope in misery,
frustration, or fear. Look upon your situation—personal,
domestic, career, mental, emotional, spiritual—as having significance within that purpose, as teaching you some specific
lesson or telling you what to do or not to do.

XVI.27.20

If the divine activity ceases in one universe it continues at
the same time in another. If our World-Mind returns to its
source in the end, there are other World-Minds and other
worlds which continue. Creation is a thing without beginning and without end, but there are interludes and periods
of rest just as there are in the individual's own life in and
outside the body.

XVI.27.30

What I termed in *The Wisdom of the Overself* 'an inner necessity' as being responsible for this self-activity of World-Mind

in bringing forth the universe needs, I now see, some clarification if it is not to be incorrectly understood. It is the nature
of World-Mind to be passive by turns, just as it is the nature
of animals and humans to be active on waking, at rest when
sleeping. In this nature, there is embedded a desire to express
something of itself in the cosmos. But the desire is not for
its own benefit, for the Perfect has nothing to gain. In all
manifested creatures, desire seeks self-benefit, obvious or hidden; not so in the World-Mind. Its activity exists only for
the benefit of this multitude of creatures.

XVI.26.21-2

The management of human affairs, the values of human society, and the operations of human faculties are basic influences
which necessarily shape human ideas or beliefs about divine
existence which, being on a totally different and transcendental level of experience, does not correspond to those concepts. The biggest of these mistakes is about the world's
creation. A picture or plan is supposed to arise in the Divine
Mind and then the Divine Will operates on something called
Matter (or, with more up-to-date human knowledge, called
Energy) to fashion the world and its inhabitants. In short,
first the thought, then, by stages, the thing is brought into
existence. A potter works like this on clay, but his mind and
power are not transcendental. The Divine Mind is its own
substance and its own energy; its thoughts are creative of
these things. Not only so but the number of universes possible is infinite. Not only this, but they are infinitely different, as though infinite self-expression were being sought.
The human understanding may reel at the idea, but creation has never had a beginning nor an end: it is eternal. Nor
can it ever come to an end (despite rhythmic intervals of
pause), for the Infinite Being can never express itself fully
in a finite number of these forms of expression.

XVI.25.5

Thus the World-Mind originates our experience for us but
we ourselves mould it. It supplies the karmic-forces material

and we as individuals supply the space-time shape which this material takes. Thus there is a union of the individual with the universal.

XVI.25.5–6

Whether we think of this mysterious origin as manifesting itself in waves of energy or in particles of the same force, it is and must be there for the deeply reflective atomic scientist. Whether we think of it as God the Creative Universal Mind or as God the inaccessible all-transcending Mind remote from human communion, it is and must be there for the intuitive. But in both cases this entire universe is but a thought in the Universal Mind. Every object and every creature is simultaneously included in this thought: therefore every human being too. Through this relationship it is possible for a man to attain some kind of communion with IT. This is what the quest is all about.

XVI.27.27

In all these studies the principal concept should be returned to again and again: the entire universe, everything—objects and creatures—is in Mind. I hold all the objects of my experience in *my* consciousness but I myself am held, along with them, in an incredibly greater consciousness, the World-Mind's.

XVI.25.12

No mortal may penetrate the mystery of the ultimate mind in its own nature—which means in its static inactive being. The Godhead is not only beyond human conception but also beyond mystic perception. But Mind in its active dynamic state, that is, the World-Mind, and rather its ray in us called the Overself, *is* within the range of human perception, communion, and even union. It is this that the mystic really finds when he believes that he has found God.

XVI.25.13

We exist always in utter dependence on the Universal Mind. Man and God may meet and mingle in his periods of supreme exaltation, he may feel the sacred presence within himself to the utmost degree, but he does not thereby abolish all the distinctions between them absolutely. For he arrives at the knowledge of the timeless spaceless divine infinitude after a process of graded personal effort, whereas the World-Mind's knowledge of itself has forever been what it was, is and shall be, above all processes and beyond all efforts.

XVI.26.10-11

The World-Idea is self-existent. It is unfolded in time and by time; it is the basis of the universe and reflected in the human being. It is the fundamental pattern of both and provides the fundamental meaning of human life.

XVI.25.24

Whenever I have written that the higher individuality is a part of the divine World-Mind, this is so only from the ordinary human standpoint looking upwards. But from the ultimate one, it is not so, for the World-Mind is not the sum total of a number of parts. It cannot be divided into them. This is why I prefer to use the phrase 'rooted in the World-Mind'.

XVI.25.29-30

There is metaphysically no such thing as a human appearance of God, as the Infinite Mind brought down into finite flesh. This error is taught as a sacred truth by the Bahais in their Manifestation doctrine, by the Christians in the Incarnation doctrine, and by the Hindus in the Avatar doctrine. God cannot be born in the flesh, cannot take a human incarnation. If He could so confine Himself, He would cease to be God. For how could the Perfect, the Incomprehensible, and the Inconceivable become the imperfect, the comprehensible, and the conceivable?

Yet there is some fire behind this smoke. From time to time, someone is born predestined to give a spiritual impulse to a particular people, area, or age. He is charged with a special mission of teaching and redemption and is imbued with special power from the universal intelligence to enable him to carry it out. He must plant seeds which grow slowly into trees to carry fruit that will feed millions of unborn people. In this sense he is different from and, if you like, superior to anyone else who is also inspired by the Overself. But this difference or superiority does not alter his human status, does not make him more than a man still, however divinely used and power-charged he may be. Such a man will claim no essential superiority over other men; on the contrary, he will plainly admit that they, too, may attain the same state of inspiration which he possesses. Hence Muhammed confessed, repeatedly: 'I am only a human being like unto yourselves. But revelations are made to me.' And the tenth Sikh guru declared, 'Those who call me the Supreme Lord will go to hell.' No human temple can receive the Infinite Essence within its confining walls. No mortal man has ever been or could ever be the Incarnation of the all-transcending Godhead. No earthly flesh or human intelligence has the right to identify itself with the unknowable principle. Only minds untrained in the metaphysics of truth could accept the contrary belief. The widespread character of this belief evidences how few have ever had such a training, and the widespread character of the corruptions and troubles which have always followed in the train of such man-worship, evidences it as a fallacy.

XVI.25.10-11

If it is wiser and humbler to leave some mystery at the bottom of all our intellectual understanding of life than to indulge in self-deceiving finality about it, then it is no less wiser and humbler to acknowledge the ultimate mystery at the heart of all our immediate mystical experience of life. The mystic's claim to know God when he knows only the deepest part of his own self, is his particular kind of vanity. Whatever terminous and transcendental consciousness he may discover there, something ever remains beyond it lost in utter inscrutability. The World-Mind is impenetrable by human power. This agnostic conclusion does not, however, touch the validity of the mystic's more legitimate claim, that the human soul *is* knowable and that an unshakeable union with it is attainable.

XVI.28.25

That which transcends even the highest of the gods, even World-Mind, is unthinkable and unimaginable. Therefore is it without name or form, beyond all contact with the senses, beginningless and endless, neither growing nor diminishing, indestructible, free from any relations or comparisons—this is the Undefinable Mystery of Mysteries. Let no one seek it, for he cannnot find IT. But he can know that it is there and, through its manifestations, the Gods, worship IT.

XVI.25.3–4

The innermost being of man and the cosmos is ever at rest, and single. The incarnate being of both is ever in movement, and dual. The inner is the Real, Changeless; the other is the Appearance, and subject to the play of two opposed but inter-penetrating active forces. Because it is the quintessence of consciousness and intelligence, I call the first Mind. It is without shape, infinite and untouchable by man, but because it *is*, universes are able to appear, expand, disintegrate, and reincarnate. This activity is directly due to the agency of the first entity to appear, which I call World-Mind. From the latter flows ceaselessly the energy which is at the heart of every atom, the life-force which is at the heart of every man. World-Mind and Mind are for us the twin sides—a crude but simple, understandable metaphor—of God. The human being draws breath, exists, and thinks with awareness only because of this relationship. If he declares himself an atheist, sees himself only as an animal, rejects any divine basis to his mind, he testifies thereby to a failure on his own part: he has failed to seek and find, or because of prejudice—that is, of prejudgement—has sought wrongly. Jesus gave two helps in this matter: seek the kingdom of heaven *first*, and seek it *within*. It is open to anyone to test this truth that he is related to God. But if he does not bring certain qualities into the work, such as patience and humility, the going may be too hard, the result disappointing.

XVI.28.7

When Mind concentrates itself into the World-Mind, it establishes a focus. However vast, it goes out of its own unlimited condition, it passes from the true Infinite to the pseudo-Infinite. Consequently the World-Mind, being occupied with its cosmos, cannot be regarded as possessed of the absolute character of Pure Mind. For what is its work but a movement of imagination? And where in the ineffable absolute is there room for either work or imagination? The one would break its eternal stillness, the other would veil its unchangeable reality. This of course it can never do, for Being can never become Non-Being. But it can send forth an emanation from itself. Such an emanation is the World-Mind. Through its prolonged contemplation of the cosmos Mind thus becomes a fragment of itself, bereft of its own undifferentiated unbroken unity. Nevertheless the World-Mind, through its deputy the Overself, is still for humans the highest possible goal.

XVI.28.9

The Mind's first expression is the Void. The second and succeeding is the Light, that is, the World-Mind. This is followed by the third, the World-Idea. Finally comes the fourth, manifestation of the world itself.

XVI.28.9

The Supreme Godhead is unindividualized. The World-Mind is individuated (but not personalized) into emanated Overselves. The Overself is an individual, but not a person. The ego is personal.

XVI.28.9

What is the meaning of the words 'the Holy Trinity'? The Father is the absolute and ineffable Godhead, Mind in its ultimate being. The Son is the soul of the universe, that is, the World-Mind. The Holy Ghost is the soul of each individual, that is, the Overself. The Godhead is one and indivisible and not multiform and can never divide itself up into three personalities.

XVI.28.4

Absolute mind is the actuality of human life and the plenitude of universal existence. Apart from Mind they could not even come into existence, and separated from it they could not continue to exist. Their truth and being are in It. But it would be utterly wrong to imagine the Absolute as the sum total of all finite beings and individual beings. The absolute is not the integral of all its visible aspects. It is the unlimited, the boundless void within which millions of universes may appear and disappear ceaselessly and unendingly but yet leave It unaffected. The latter do not exhaust even one millionth of its being.

XVI.27.32

Manifestation implies the necessity of manifesting. But it might be objected that any sort of necessity existing in the divine equally implies its insufficiency. The answer is that the number One may become aware of itself as being one only by becoming aware of the presence of Two—itself and another. But the figure Nought is under no compulsion. Here we have a mathematical hint towards understanding the riddle of manifestation. Mind as Void is the supreme inconceivable unmanifesting ultimate whereas the World-Mind is forever throwing forth the universe-series as a second, an 'other' wherein it becomes self-aware.

XVI.27.32

It would, however, be a mistake to consider the World-Mind

as one entity and Mind as another separate from it. It would be truer to consider World-Mind as the active function of Mind. Mind cannot be separated from its powers. The two are one. In its quiescent state it is simply Mind. In its active state it is World-Mind. Mind in its innermost transcendent nature is the inscrutable mystery of Mysteries but when expressing itself in act and immanent in the universe, it is the World-Mind. We may find in the attributes of the manifested God—that is, the World-Mind—the only indications of the quality, existence, and character of the unmanifest Godhead that it is possible for man to comprehend. All this is a mystery which is and perhaps forever will remain an incomprehensible paradox.

XVI.27.33

Mind active and mind in quiescence are not two separate beings, but two aspects of one and the same being as they appear to human inquiry. Mind active expresses itself in the heart of man as his higher self and in the universe as the World-Mind.

XVI.27.31

As Mind, it is beyond all the relativities of this world, beyond time and space, human thought and human imagination. As World-Mind it is immanent in the world itself, the Lord of the All, the God whom men worship, yet cyclic in Its existences.

XVI.27.31

The notion of a Personal God includes a truth and an error. So far as there is a World-Mind, manifesting along with a world itself, the notion is true. But so far as there is only the Unique, the One without a Second, both are appearances, phenomena out of the Noumenon. In the case of the world, it appears in time out of the Timeless; but in the case of the World-Mind, all times are embraced in its Duration. Yet it too withdraws into its other aspect, Mind—only.

XVI.28.14-15

The Real is forever and unalterably the same, whether it be the unmanifest Void or the manifested world. It has never been born and consequently can never die. It cannot divide itself into different 'realities' with different space-time levels or multiply itself beyond its own primal oneness. It cannot evolve or diminish, improve or deteriorate. Whereas everything else exists in dependence upon Mind and exists for a limited time, however prolonged, and therefore has only a relative existence, Mind is the absolute, the unique, the ultimate reality because with all its innumerable manifestations in the universe it has never at any moment ceased to be itself. Only its appearances suffer change because they are in time and space, never itself, which is out of time and space. The divisions of time into past and present and future are meaningless here; we may speak of its 'everness'. The truth about it is timeless, as no scientific truth could ever be, in the sense that whatever fate the universe undergoes its own ultimate significance remains unchanged. If the Absolute appears *to us* as the first in the time-series, as the First Cause of the Universe, this is only true from our limited standpoint. It is in fact only our human idea. The human mind can take into itself the truth of transcendental being only by taking out of itself the screens of time, space and person. For being eternally self-existence, reality is utterly timeless. Space divisions are equally unmeaning in its 'Be-ness'. The Absolute is both everywhere and nowhere. It cannot be considered in spatial terms. Even the word 'infinite' is really such a term. If it is used here because no other is available, let it be clearly understood, then, that it is used merely as a suggestive metaphor. If the infinite did not include the finite then it would be less than infinite. It is erroneous to make them both mutually exclusive. The finite alone must exclude the infinite from its experience but not vice versa. In the same way the infinite Duration does not exclude finite time.

XVI.28.17

If Mind is to be regarded aright, we must put out of our

thought even the notion of the cosmic Ever-Becoming. But
to do this is to enter a virtual Void? Precisely. When we take
away all the forms of external physical existence and all the
differences of internal mental existence, what we get is an
utter emptiness of being which can hardly be differentiated
after we have taken away its features and individualities, its
finite times and finite distances. There is then nothing but
a great void. What is the nature of this void? It is pure
Thought. It is out of this empty Thought that the fullness
of the universe has paradoxically evolved. Hence it is said
that the world's reality is secondary whereas Mind's reality
is primary. In the Void the hidden oneness of things is dis-
engaged from the things themselves. Silence therefore is not
merely the negation of sound but rather the element in
which, as Carlyle said, great things fashion themselves. It
is the supreme storehouse of power.

XVI.28.17

There is here no form to be perceived, no image born of
the senses to be worshipped, no oracular utterance to be
listened for, and no emotional ecstasy to be revelled in. Hence
the Chinese sage, Lao Tsu, said: 'In eternal non-existence I
look for the spirituality of things!' The philosopher perceives
that there is no such thing as creation out of nothing for
the simple reason that Mind is eternally and universally
present. 'Nothing' is merely an appearance. Here indeed
there is neither time nor space. It is like a great silent boundless circle wherein no life seems to stir, no consciousness
seems to be at work, and no activity is in sway. Yet the seer
will know by a pure insight which will grip his consciousness as it has never been gripped before, that here indeed
is the root of all life, all consciousness, and all activity. But
how it is so is as inexplicable intellectually as what its nature
is. With the Mind the last word of human comprehension
is uttered. With the Mind the last world of possible being
is explored. But whereas the utterance is comprehensible by
his consciousness, the speaker is not. It is a Silence which
speaks but what it says is only that it IS; more than that none
can hear.

XVI.28.37

Neither the senses nor the intellect can tell us anything about
the intrinsic nature of this Infinite Mind. Nevertheless we
are not left in total ignorance about it. From its manifestation, the cosmos, we may catch a hint of its Intelligence.
From its emanation, the soul, we may catch more than a
hint of its Beneficence. 'More than' I say, because the emanation may be felt within us as our very being whereas the
manifestation is outside us and is apart.

XVI.28.37-8

The topic with which all such metaphysical thinking should
end after it has pondered on mentalism is that out of which
the thinking principle itself arises—Mind—and it should be
considered under its aspect as the one reality. When this
intellectual understanding is brought within one's own
experience as fact, when it is made as much one's own as
a bodily pain, then it becomes direct insight. Such thinking
is the most profitable and resultful in which he can engage,
for it brings the student to the very portal of Mind where
it stops activity by itself and where the differentiation of ideas
disappears. As the mental muscles strain after this concept
of the Absolute, the Ineffable and Infinite, they lose their
materialist rigidity and become more sensitive to intimations
from the Overself. When thinking is able to reach such a
profound depth that it attains utter impersonality and calm
universality, it is able to approach the fundamental principle of its own being. When hard thinking reaches a culminating point, it then voluntarily destroys itself. Such an
attainment of course can take place deep within the innermost recesses of the individual's consciousness alone.

XVI.28.38

He will arrive at the firm unshakeable conviction that there
is an inward reality behind all existence. If he wishes he may
go farther still and seek to translate the intellectual idea of
this reality into a conscious fact. In that case the comprehension that in the quest of pure Mind he is in quest of that

which is alone the Supreme Reality in this entire universe, must possess him. The mystery of Mind is a theme upon which no aspirant can ever reflect enough: first, because of its importance, and second, because of its capacity to unfold his latent spirituality. He will doubtless feel cold on these lofty peaks of thought, but in the end he will find a heavenly reward whilst still on earth. We are not saying that something of the nature of mind as we humans know it is the supreme reality of the universe, but only that it is more like that reality than anything else we know of and certainly more like it than what we usually call by the name of 'matter'. The simplest way to express this is to say that Reality is of the nature of our mind rather than of our body, although it is Mind transcending familiar phases and raised to infinity. It is the ultimate being, the highest state. This is the Principle which forever remains what it was and will be. It is in the universe and yet the universe is in it too. It never evolves, for it is outside time. It has not shape, for it is outside space. It is beyond man's consciousness, for it is beyond both his thoughts and sense-experience, yet all consciousness springs mysteriously out of it. Nevertheless man may enter into its knowledge, may enter into its Void, so soon as he can drop his thoughts, let go his sense-experience, but keep his sense of being. Then he may understand what Jesus meant when saying: 'He that loseth his life shall find it.' Such an accomplishment may appear too spectral to be of any use to his matter-of-fact generation. What is their madness will be his sanity. He will know there is reality where they think there is nothingness.

7

THE SAGE

XVI.25.19

An important warning is needed here. Wherever the idea of agnostic mysticism has been supported, the idea that there is no possibility of knowing the Absolute and so no communication of such knowledge, the reference is to ordinary human intellect. No positive result can come of its investigation into that which transcends it. But what intellect unaided cannot know, intuition—a higher faculty—can. It can discover its point of contact with the Absolute—its higher individuality, the Overself, even though it can go no farther and penetrate the Absolute. When intuition becomes active in this matter, it may or may not take the shape of a mystical experience. When it is developed by philosophic training, it expands into insight.

XVI.25.24

The teaching of a higher individuality needs to be correctly understood. It is not that a separate one exists for each physical body. The consciousness which normally identifies itself with the body—that is, the ego—when looking upward in highest devotion or inward in deepest meditation, comes to the point of contact with universal being, World-Mind. This point is its own higher self, the divine deputy within its own being. But if devotion or meditation is carried still further, to the very utmost possible stretch of consciousness, the point itself merges into its source. At this moment the man is his source. But—'Man shall not see My face and live!' He

returns eventually to earth-consciousness, where he must
follow out its requirements. Yet the knowledge of what he
is *in essence* remains. The presence of the deputy is always
there meanwhile, always felt. It may fittingly be called his
higher individuality.

XVI.25.38-9

Is insight achieved gradually or suddenly, as the Zen Buddhists claim? Here again both claims are correct, if taken
together as parts of a larger and fuller view. We have to begin
by cultivating intuitive feelings. These come to us infre-
quently at first and so the process is a gradual and long one.
Eventually, we reach a point, a very advanced point, where
the ego sees its own limitation, perceives its helplessness and
dependence, realizes that it cannot lift itself up into the final
illuminations. It should then surrender itself wholly to the
Overself and cast its further development on the mercy and
Grace of the power beyond it. It will then have to go through
a waiting period of seeming inactivity, spiritual stagnation,
and inability to feel the fervour of devotion which it formerly felt. This is a kind of dark night of the soul. Then, slowly,
it begins to come out of this phase, which is often accompanied by mental depression and emotional frustration, into
a higher phase where it feels utterly resigned to the will of
God or destiny, calm and peaceful in the sense of accepting
that higher will and not in any joyous sense, patiently waiting for the time when the infinite wisdom will bring it what
it once sought so ardently but what it is now as detached
from as it is detached from wordly ambitions. After this phase
there will come suddenly unexpectedly and in the dead of
night, as it were, a tremendous Realization of the egoless
state, a tremendous feeling of liberation from itself as it has
known itself, a tremendous awareness of the infinitude,
universality, and intelligence of life. With that, new perceptions into the Laws of the cosmos will suddenly unfold
themselves. The seeker must thus pass from intuition into
insight.

XVI.25.47

The understanding that everything is illusive is not the final one. It is an essential stage but only a stage. Ultimately you will understand that the form and separateness of a thing are illusory, but the thing-in-itself is not. *That* out of which these forms appear is not different from them, hence Reality is one and the same in all things. This is the paradox of life and a sharp mind is needed to perceive it. However, to bring beginners out of their earthly attachments, we have to teach first the illusoriness of the world, and then raise them to a higher level of understanding and show that the world is not apart from the Real. *That Thou Art* unifies everything in essence. But the final realization cannot be got by stilling the mind, only by awakening it into full vigour again after yogic peace has been attained and then letting its activity cease of its own accord when thought merges voluntarily into insight. When that is done, you know the limitations of both yoga and enquiry as successive stages. Whoever realizes this truth does not divorce from matter—as most yogis do—but realizes non-difference from it. Hence we call this highest path the 'yoga of non-duality'. But to reach it one has to pass through the 'yoga of philosophical knowledge'. Christian Science caught glimpses of the higher truth but Mrs Eddy got her facts and fancies confused together.

XII.21.129

The world looks just as it did before; being understood for what it is—a thought-series—does not alter its appearance. The sage's perception of it is like other men's; his senses function like theirs; but he knows that his experience of it depends on the ever-presence of Consciousness; *he is never without this awareness.* This is the large first difference.

XIII.21.136

Whatever becomes an object to consciousness cannot be the conscious self which notes it as an object. Every thought, therefore, even the thought of the person, is such an object. The real self must consequently inhere in a consciousness which transcends the person and which can be nothing other than pure consciousness itself. The keen insight of the Chinese sages perceived this and hence they used the term *Ko*, which means 'to be aware', as representing the transcendental knowledge of real being, and the same term, which also means 'he who is aware', as representing a man like the Buddha who is possessed of such knowledge.

XIII.21.137

In ordinary experience consciousness is not found by itself, independent of what it holds, separate from what it perceives and experiences, distinct from the things given to it by the world outside. That is to say, it is not isolated from its contents but always inclusive of them. And not only is it connected together with physical objects but also with different ideas that are merely thought about, with reasonings and imaginings. There is further evidence of this relationship to be found when we turn from the waking state to the sleeping one. When this is really deep, without dreams, there is no world and there are no imaginings. At such a time consciousness does not exist. When thoughts come into being within a man, the world comes into being for him. When they die down, he loses his consciousness and his world too. But the opening of this paragraph was qualified by the three words 'in ordinary experience'. For a few men, consciousness without thoughts has become a practical realization: for the whole race of men, it remains in the future as an evolutionary possibility. These adepts find Consciousness-in-itself *is* the reality out of which thoughts rise, including the world-thought. It is not easy to adduce evidence for this since these are events in private personal biography, not scientifically verifiable.

XV.23.229

So many conversations on the words of Jesus have taken his sentence 'I and my Father are one' to mean a kind of union like marriage. But they overlook the fact that married couples still remain couples, still express the number two. Jesus did not say, 'I and my Father are two.' The number one is definitely not two. For Jesus found, as every other man who attains that stage of consciousness finds, that when contemplating the Infinite Life-Power (which he named the Father) he himself vanished. There was then no other consciousness except that of the Infinite itself. For That was the substratum of his own 'I'. But what happened in his contemplation two thousand years ago still happens today; the same discovery is made when the illusion of egoity vanishes.

VIII.12.61

Unforgettable as the finding of secret wealth was the day when this Overself chose to make itself known to me. For I had reached a crisis in my life and could go no farther if this troubling of the air with harsh thoughts was not put right in the only way it could be put right. Many are the adventures and manifold incidents that have befallen me since that time, both of woe and weal. But now they do not matter, nor do I deem them worth the trouble of recording. For the mists that lay about me began to die away, and I came to know that man does not walk alone. The Overself *is ever with him*. As the years unfolded the dark curtains of the future, a strange quiescence stole upon the heart when it placed its life upon the altar of obedience, and when it grew to accept each day as freely as the wandering nomad accepts the pitiless desert in which he was born. It then cast the shroud of care that enveloped it and turned from the tomb of unsatisfied desire. So I came to wrap myself round with the silken mantle of secret hidden Beauty and sought to let no bitter brooding, no storm of passion touch it.

XV.23.181

Noises and sights may be still present in the background of consciousness but the pull and fascination of the inner being will be strong enough to hold him and they will not be able to move his attention away from it. This, of course, is an advanced state; but once mastered and familiar, it must yield to the next one. Here, as if passing from this waking world to a dream one, there is a slip-over into universal space, incredibly vast and totally empty. Consciousness is there but, as he discovers later, this too is only a phase through which it passes. Where, and when, will it all end? When Consciousness is led—by Grace—to itself, beyond its states, phases, and conditions where man, at last, is fit to meet God.

XV.23.219

He is to look for no support elsewhere and no light. Evidently the passage to such a unique position may frighten some aspirants to such a degree that they refuse to traverse it. This is not an ordinary kind of courage which is required here. All that ties him to his nature as a human being, to his very existence, must be let go. Nothing less than annihilation seems to confront him. Indeed, afterwards, when the experience is over, he thinks to himself that it was really 'a kind of dying'. He had been swallowed by death but disgorged again later. He had slipped into it so imperceptibly, so unconsciously, and so suddenly, that all this became known only after it was over.

VI.9.165

With reference to your second point, fate and free will, what I meant was that ordinarily man is subject to fate simultaneously with the fact that he is also operating his will. The two factors are ever present. But as the same fate was made by him in former lives, and he had the freedom to make it as he wished, ultimately there is freedom. You ask why 'the dilemma is self-created and does not exist in Nature?' I plead guilty to having been deliberately obscure. I could not explain the problem without going at length into the esoteric philosophy, the study of which proves that where everything is ONE the individual will and fate fall out of consideration from the standpoint of the ONE, or Nature. The Sage is the man who has realized this oneness and hence for him such questions do not arise.

XIII.19.72-3

When in deep sleep we have absolutely no sense of Time's existence at all. We are then in eternity! When we become thoroughly convinced of the illusoriness of time, and make this conviction a settled attitude, eternity reveals itself even during the waking state. This is life in the Overself. This is not the same as totalizing the past, present and future; all those belong to illusion. This realization gives perfect peace.

XV.24.69

To be at peace means to be empty of all desires—a state the ordinary man often ridicules as inhuman or dismisses as impossible. The spiritual seeker goes farther and understands better, so he desires to be without desire—but only to a limited extent. Moreover, some of his desires may be hidden from consciousness. Only the sage, by which I do not mean the saint, is completely free from desires because the empty void thus created is completely filled by the Overself.

XIV.22.82

It is a state of pure intelligence but without the working of the intellectual and ideational process. Its product may be named intuition. There are no automatically conceived ideas present in it, no habitually followed ways of thinking. It is pure, clear stillness.

XIV.22.81

This is the 'Undivided Mind' where experience as subject and object, as ego and the world, or as higher self and lower self, does not break consciousness.

XVI.25.47

The illuminate is conscious of both the ultimate unity and the immediate multiplicity of the world. This is a paradox. But his permanent resting place while he is dealing with others is at the junction-point of duality and unity so that he is ready at any moment to absorb his attention in either phase.

XVI.25.51

Sahaja samadhi is the awareness of Awareness, whether appearing as thoughts or not, whether accompanied by bodily activity or not. But *nirvikalpa samadhi* is solely the awareness of Awareness.

XVI.25.51

What is the difference between the state of deepest contemplation, which the Hindus call *nirvikalpa samadhi*, and that which they call *sahaja samadhi*? The first is only a temporary experience, that is it begins and ends but the man actually experiences an uplift of consciousness, he gains a new and higher outlook. But *sahaja* is continuous unbroken realization that as Overself he always was, is, and shall be. It is not a feeling that something new and higher has been gained. What is the absolute test which distinguishes one condition from the other, since both are awareness of the Overself? In *nirvikalpa* the ego vanishes but reappears when the ordinary state is resumed: hence it has only been lulled, even though it has been slightly weakened by the process. In *sahaja* the ego is rooted out once and for all! It not only vanishes, but it cannot reappear.

XVI.25.49

Paras on *sahaja*: It is *wrong* to use the illustration of a camera shutter—the image getting larger or vaguer or smaller and sharper as it opens or closes—for attention focused on *nirvikalpa* in meditation or spread out in *sahaja* in the wakeful state. The correct illustration is this: the stillness is being experienced at the centre of a circle, the thoughts revolve around it at the circumference. But the degree of Stillness remains just as much in outer activity as in meditation.

XV.24.78

In *sahaja* we'll possess an imperturbable temperament; we'll possess human feeling but not be subject to the vicissitudes, excitements, and oscillations of human feeling. The mind will always be composed, because it will be held by the divine presence.

XVI.25.52

I am an Advaitin on the fundamental point of nonduality of the Real, but I am unable to limit myself to most Advaitins' practical view of *samadhi* and *sahaja*. Here I stand with Chinese Zen (*Ch'an*), especially as I was taught and as explained by the Sixth Patriarch, Hui Neng. He warns against turning meditation into a narcotic, resulting in a pleasant passivity. He went so far as to declare: 'It is quite unnecessary to stay in monasteries. Only let your mind . . . function in freedom . . . let it abide nowhere.' And in this connection he later explains: 'To be free from attachment to all outer objects is true meditation. To meditate means to realize thus tranquillity of Essence of Mind.'

On *samadhi*, he defines it as a mind self-trained to be unattached amid objects, resting in tranquillity and peace. On *sahaja*, it is thorough understanding of the truth about reality and a penetration into and through delusion, to one's Essence of Mind. The Indian notion of *sahaja* makes it the extension of *nirvikalpa samadhi* into the active everyday state. But the *Ch'an* conception of *nirvikalpa samadhi* differs from this; it does not seek deliberately to eliminate thoughts, although that may often happen of its own accord through identification with the true Mind, but to eliminate the personal feelings usually attached to them, that is, to remain unaffected by them because of this identification.

Ch'an does not consider *sahaja* to be the fruit of yoga meditation alone, nor of understanding alone, but of a combination seemingly of both. It is a union of reason and intuition. It is an awakening once and for all. It is not attained in *nirvikalpa* and then to be held as long as possible. It is not something, a state alternately gained and lost on numerous occasions, but gradually expanded as it is clung to. It is a single awakening that enlightens the man so that he never returns to ignorance again. He has awakened to his divine essence, his source in Mind, as an all day and every day self-identification. It has come by itself, effortlessly.

XVI.25.10

In my alleged claim that every human being can develop the divinity within himself, I do not mean that we poor mortals can ever rise to the stature of the Almighty, and I completely concur with the warning of Baha'u'llah against man's attempting to 'join partners with God'. I mean only that we have within us something that is linked with and related to God: it is our higher self, the discovery of and union with which represents the limit of our possible attainment.

XVI.25.10

We may dwell in mystical inner fellowship with God but we may not become as God. Those who proclaim such false self-deification needlessly make a grotesquely exaggerated statement of what is already by itself a sufficiently tremendous truth.

XVI.28.36

Let us not deceive ourselves and dishonour the Supreme Being by thinking that we know anything at all about IT. We know nothing. The intellect may formulate conceptions, the intuition may give glimpses; but these are our human reactions to IT. Even the sage, who has attained a harmony with his Overself, has found only the godlike *within himself*. Yes, it is certainly the Light, but it is so *for him*, for the human being. He still stands as much outside the divine Mystery as everyone else. The difference is that whereas they stand in darkness he stands in this Light.

XVI.25.59

It is a fallacy to think that this displacement of the lower self brings about its complete substitution by the infinite and absolute Deity. This fallacy is an ancient and common one in mystical circles and leads to fantastic declarations of self-deification. If the lower self is displaced, it is not destroyed. It lives on but in strict subordination to the higher one, the Overself, the divine soul of man; and it is this latter, not the divine world-principle, which is the true displacing element.

XVI.25.46

There is some confusion on this point in the minds of many students. On attaining enlightenment a man does not attain omniscience. At most, he may receive a revelation of the inner operations of life and Nature, of the higher laws governing life and man. That is, he may also become a seer and find a cosmogony presented to his gaze. But the actuality in a majority of cases is that he attains enlightenment only, not cosmogonical seership.

XV.23.233

When we comprehend that the pure essence of mind is reality, then we can also comprehend the rationale of the higher yoga which would settle attention in pure thought itself rather than in finite thoughts. When this is done the mind becomes vacant, still, and utterly undisturbed. This grand calm of nonduality comes to the philosophic yogi alone and is not to be confused with the lower-mystical experience of emotional ecstasy, clairvoyant vision, and inner voice. For in the latter the ego is present as its enjoyer, whereas in the former it is absent because the philosophic discipline has led to its denial. The lower type of mystic must make a special effort to gain his ecstatic experience, but the higher type finds it arises spontaneously without personal effort at all. The first is in the realm of duality, whilst the second has realized nonduality.

XVI.28.47

Without keeping steadily in view this original mentalness of things and hence their original oneness with self and Mind, the mystic must naturally get confused if not deceived by what he takes to be the opposition of Spirit and Matter. The mystic looks within, to self; the materialist looks without, to world. And each misses what the other finds. But to the philosopher neither of these is primary. He looks to that Mind of which both self and world are but manifestations and in which he finds the manifestations also. It is not enough for him to receive, as the mystic receives, fitful and occasional illuminations from periodic meditation. He relates this intellectual understanding to his further discovery got during mystical self-absorption in the Void that the reality of his own self is Mind. Back in the world once more he studies it again under this further light, confirms that the manifold world consists ultimately of mental images, conjoins with his full metaphysical understanding that it is simply Mind in manifestation, and thus comes to comprehend that it is essentially one with the same Mind which he experiences in self-absorption. Thus his insight actualizes, experiences, this Mind-in-itself as and not apart from the sensuous world whereas the mystic divides them. With insight, the sense of oneness does not destroy the sense of difference but both remain strangely present, whereas with the ordinary mystical perception each cancels the other. The myriad forms which make up the picture of this world will not disappear as an essential characteristic of reality nor will his awareness of them or his traffic with them be affected. Hence he possesses a firm and final attainment wherein he will permanently possess the insight into pure Mind even in the midst of physical sensations. He sees everything in this multitudinous world as being but the Mind itself as easily as he can see nothing, the imageless Void, as being but the Mind itself, whenever he cares to turn aside into self-absorption. He sees both the outer faces of all men and the inner depths of his own self as being but the Mind itself. Thus he experiences the unity of all existence; not intermittently but at every moment he knows the Mind as ultimate. This is the philosophic or final realization. It is as permanent as the mystic's is transient. Whatever he does or refrains from doing, whatever he experiences or fails to experience, he gives up all discriminations between reality and appearance, between truth and illusion, and lets his insight function freely as his thoughts select and cling to nothing. He experiences the miracle of undifferentiated being, the wonder of undifferenced unity. The artificial man-made frontiers melt away. He sees his fellow men as inescapably and inherently divine as they are, not merely as the mundane creatures they believe they are, so that any traces of an ascetical holier-than-thou attitude fall completely away from him.

XV.23.239-40

Paradoxically, it is in the trancelike state of self-absorption that the degree of passing away from the personal self is completely achieved. But when nature reasserts herself and brings the mystic back to his normal condition, she brings him back to the personality too. For without some kind of self-identification with his body, his thoughts, and his feelings, he could not attend to personal duties and necessities at all.

XVI.28.44

If you believe that you have had the ultimate experience, it is more likely that you had an emotional, or mental, or mystic one. The authentic thing does not *enter* consciousness. You do not know that it has transpired. You discover it is already here only by looking back at what you were and contrasting it with what you now are; or when others recognize it in you and draw attention to it; or when a situation arises which throws up your real status. It is a permanent fact, not a brief mystic 'glimpse'.

XIII.19.56

It is the presence of the physical ego in the wakeful state that paralyses all spiritual awareness therein. It is the absence of the personal and physical ego in the deep sleep state that paralyses all material awareness therein, too. By keeping it

out and yet keeping in wakefulness, the transcendental consciousness is able to provide the requisite condition for an
unbroken spiritual awareness that is not only superior to the
three states but continues its own existence behind theirs.

XIII.19.26

His awareness of the relativity of things relieves the philosopher of any compulsion to identify himself with any particular viewpoint. His liberation from dogma enables him
to take the viewpoint which best suits the circumstances.
This does not at all mean that chaos will enter into his affairs,
insincerity into his attitudes, and anarchy into his morals.
He is safeguarded from such perils by the link he has established with the Overself's wisdom and immeasurable goodness.

XV.24.98

The whole of one's aim should be to keep the mind in an
unbroken rest permanently, while using the intellect whenever necessary in an automatic manner to attend to external duties. 'Does not that destroy the efficiency of the
intellect?' it may be objected. No—only its selfishness is destroyed. Do the hands lose their efficiency because we use
them in a purely mechanical manner? Just the same, when
one unites with God he regards himself as greater than mere
intellect, which becomes for him only an instrument to deal
with the external world.

XV.24.97

The freedom which he attains is in the background of consciousness, as it were. For here he rests tranquilly in the mind-
essence alone. No separate ideas exist here, whereas the foreground is occupied by the ordinary ideas involved in human
existence. He perceives now that the value of all his former
yoga practice lay in its capacity, when success crowned it,
to enable him to approach behind the stream of ideas to
the bed on which it flowed, that is, to the mind-stuff
itself.

XIII.19.28

The illumined person must conform to the double action of nature in him, that is, to the outgoing and incoming breaths. So his illumination must be there in the mind, and here in the body. It is the two together which form the equilibrium of the double life we are called upon to live— being in the world and yet not of it. In the prolongation of the expiring breath, we not only get rid of negative thought, but also of the worldliness, the materialism of keeping to the physical alone. With the incoming breath we draw positive inspiring remembrance of the divine hidden in the void. Hence we are *there* in the mind and *here* in the body. We recognize the truth of eternity yet act in time. We see the reality of the Void, yet know that the entire universe comes forth from it.

XV.24.71

Whoever acts by becoming so pliable as to let the Overself hold his personal will, must necessarily become inwardly detached from the personal consequences of his deeds. This will be true whether those consequences be pleasant or unpleasant. Such detachment liberates him from the power of karma, which can no longer catch him in its web, for 'he' is not there. His emotional consciousness preceding an action is always enlightened and characterized by sublime composure, whereas the unenlightened man's may be characterized by motivations of self-centered desire, ambition, fear, hope, greed, passion, dislike, or even hate—all of which are karma-making.

VI.9.140

Karma comes into play only if the karmic impression is strong enough to survive. In the case of the sage, because he treats life like a dream, because he sees through it as appearance, all his experiences are on the surface only. His deep inner mind remains untouched by them. Therefore he makes no karma from them, therefore he is able when passing out of the body at death to be finished with the round of birth and death forever.

VI.9.109

Only the sage perceives with deadly clarity how like the dust blown hither and thither is the weary labour of their days; how frail are the timbers of the ships which men send out, laden with their self-spun hopes and fears; how dream-like are their entire lives.

XIV.22.87

The Overself does not evolve and does not progress. These are activities which belong to time and space. It is nowhere in time and nowhere in space. It *is* Here, in this deep beautiful and all-pervading calm, that a man finds his real identity.

XV.23.243

Those little figures and large statues of the Buddha which are to be found in some Western homes, museums, and art galleries of quality, show us perfect examples not only of the power of concentration, but also of the meaning of contemplation. For in them we behold the sage utterly absorbed in the Void's stillness, ego merged in the universal being, consciousness empty of all moving thoughts.

XV.24.49

Because he can see straight through it, because he can penetrate its true nature, reaching Reality through the Appearance that it merely is, he can deal with the world, negotiate its transactions, and experience its ups and downs all the better now that he is detached and nonchalant.

XV.24.46

Jesus did not answer when malignment and malediction were hurled upon him. Buddha kept silent when vilification and abuse were uttered against him. These great souls did not live in the ego and therefore did not care to defend it.

XV.24.103

Thoughts can be put into works, spoken and written; but the truth about Reality must remain unworded, unspoken, and unwritten. All statements about it which the intellect can grasp are merely symbolic—just clues, hints. Only in the great stillness can it be known, understood.

XV.24.103

At this point, communication by words must stop; the seer lapses into himself, into his own silent experience of the Ineffable where there is no second person.

XV.24.63–4

The peace in such a man's heart is as measureless as his trust in Infinite Mind. Indeed the peace is there because of the trust. He has no need to open the door of the future. The experience he needs or the thing he must have will, he knows, emerge from its obscurity before his eyes at the proper time. So he is patient enough to let circumstances ripen of themselves, when patience is necessary.

XV.24.45

It is not that he takes a neutral position in all controversies—he sees only too well for that—but rather that he prefers to be disinvolved and detached by attending to his own business, where alone he can do the most good!

XV.24.43

Whoever lives in the spirit lives in its perennial peace. It is a happy peace, a smiling peace, but he is not lost in it. He is aware also of the suffering which exists around him and in the world at large. In just the same way, if he is responsive to the beauty which nature offers and man creates, he is also aware of the ugliness which exists.

XV.24.76

He has gone far when he can live in this remembrance and

this presence without constraint even while occupied in the affairs of this world; when it all becomes a settled, easy, and especially *natural* attitude entirely free from superior airs, from a holier-than-thou or even a wiser-than-thou attitude. For humility grows side by side with his growth, of itself, unbidden. (How different from the arrogant egoistic pride of the self-conscious intellectual whose real worship is only himself!) By 'natural' I mean not a self-conscious thing and certainly not a forced one. It is no supernatural experience either, but human consciousness put at a better level where it has harmony with World-Idea. It is easier to withdraw from the world, where people portray so widely and so often all their inadequacies, than to return to it and apply positively what is learned during withdrawal. It is more possible for the spectator to appraise the passing show and evaluate its offerings than to come back, walk with it, keep sagehood, remain human, yet find the point of sane equilibrium between both conditions.

XV.24.31

Some people mistake philosophic calm for fatalistic resignation. This is because the philosopher will seem to endure for some situations stoically unperturbed. They do not know that where he finds that he cannot work outwardly to improve a situation, he will work inwardly to extract the utmost spiritual profit from it.

XVI.25.156

What is the sage's reaction to the cosmos? It is very different from that of the ignorant who have never asked the question. 'What am I?' and who may regard the calm visage of a Yogi as a 'frozen face'. The sage has no sense of conflict, no inner division. He has expanded his notion of self until it has embraced the universe and therefore rightly he may say 'the universe is my idea'. He may make this strange utterance because he has so expanded his understanding of mind. Lesser men may only say 'the universe is an idea'.

XIII.19.48

Although the sage withdraws with the onset of sleep from wakeful awareness, he does not withdraw from all awareness. A pleasurable and peaceful sense of impersonal being is left over. In this he rests throughout the night.

XIII.19.37

The adept not only knows when asleep that his dream-world is only mental, but he also knows when awake that his wakeful-world is also mental.

XIII.19.49

If the sage's sleep is wholly without those varied mental experiences of persons and places which manifest as dreams, then it will pass so swiftly that an entire night's sleep will take no longer than a few seconds of wakeful time.

XV.23.180

His power of abstract concentration, of withdrawing into a thought or a series of thoughts, or of having no thoughts at all, shows in the eyes, in their long-sustained stillness, their brilliance and 'not seeing' physically because focused on nothing in particular.

XVI.25.58

When it is said that we lose our individuality on entering Nirvana, words are being used loosely and faultily. So long as a man, whether he be Buddha or Hitler, has to walk, eat and work, he must use his individuality. What *is* lost by the sage is his *attachment* to individuality with its desires, hates, angers, and passions.

XV.24.31

It is not correct to believe that the stricken body of a sage suffers no pain. It is there and it is felt, but it is enclosed by a larger peace-filled consciousness. The one is a witness of the other. So pain is countered but not removed.

XIII.19.89

He lives, as I once wrote, on the pinpoint of a moment. He has no clear idea of his next move forward and less of his probable position in the future generally.

XV.24.75

The Real can't be merely static, actionless; this aspect is one of its faces, but there are two faces. The other is dynamic, ever-active. On the path, the discovery of its quiescent aspect is the first stage; this is mysticism. But the world is always confronting him and its activity has to be harmonized with inner peace. This harmonization can only be established by returning to the deserted world (while still retaining the peace) and making the second discovery—that it, too, is God active. Only then can he have unbroken peace, as before it will be intermittent. He then understands things in a different way.

XIII.21.132-3

The mind can know as a second thing, as an object, that which is outside itself. This applies to thoughts also. If it is to know anything as it really is in itself, it must unite with that object and become it, in which case the distinction of duality disappears. For instance, to know a person, one must temporarily *become* that person by uniting with him. Otherwise, all one knows of that person is the mental picture, which may not be similar to the real person. Similarly, the Ultimate Consciousness is not something to be known as a second being apart from oneself. If he knows it in that way he really knows only his mental picture of it. To know it in truth he has to enter into union with it and then the little ego disappears as a separate being but remains as part of the larger self. The wave then knows itself not only as a little wave dancing on the surface of the ocean, but also as the ocean itself. But as all the water of the ocean is ONE, it can no longer regard the millions of other waves as being, from the standpoint of ultimate truth, different from itself. To render this clearer still, during a dream he sees living men, houses, animals, and streets. Each is seen as a separate entity. But after he awakens, he understands that all these individual entities issued forth from a single source—his own mind. Therefore they were all made of the same stuff as his mind, they were non-different from it, they were not other than the mind itself. Similarly when he completes the Ultimate Path he will awaken from the illusion of world-existence and *know* that the entire experience was and is a fragmentation of his own essential being, which he now will no longer limit to the personal self, but will expand to its true nature as the universal mind. The dream will go on all the same because he is still in the flesh, but he will dream *consciously* and know exactly what is happening and what underlies it all. When this happens he cannot go on living just for purely personal aims but will have to enlarge them to include the welfare of all beings. This does not mean he will neglect his own individual welfare, but only that he will keep it in its place side by side with the welfare of others.

XV.24.100

The truth which leads a man to liberation from all illusions and enslavements is perceived in the innermost depths of his being, where he is shut off from all other men. The man who has attained to its knowledge finds himself in an exalted solitude. He is not likely to find his way out of it to the extent, and for the purpose, of enlightening his fellow men who are accustomed to, and quite at home in, their darkness unless some other propulsive force of compassion arises within him and causes him to do so.

XVI.25.136-7

Whoever has attained this blessed state would not be true to himself if he were not ardently happy to share it with others, if he were not ever ready to help them attain it too. And this desire extends universally to all without exception. He excludes none—how could he if the compassion which he feels be the real thing that comes with the realized unity of the Overself, that is, of the Christ-self, and not merely a temporary emotional masquerader! He himself could have written those noble words which Saint Paul wrote more than once in his epistles: 'In Him there cannot be Jew or Greek, Barbarian, Scythian, but all are one man in Christ Jesus.' Despite this, he soon finds that iron fetters have been placed on his feet. He finds, first, that only the few who are themselves seekers are at all interested; second, that even among this small number there are those who, because of personal dislikes, racial prejudice, social snobbery, or family antagonism, are unwilling to approach him; and third, that the mischievous agencies from occult spheres, through false reports and stimulated malice, delude a part of those who remain into creating an evil mental picture of him which is utterly unlike the actuality. For when such a man really begins to become an effective worker in this sacred cause, the evil forces begin their endeavours to pull him down and thus stop him. They may inspire human instruments with fierce jealousy or personal hatred of him, or they may try other ways. It is their task to destroy the little good that he has done or to prevent whatever good he may yet do. It is an unfortunate but historic fact that many an aspirant is carried away by the false suggestions emanating from such poisoned sources.

XVI.25.151

Bergson was right. His acute French intelligence penetrated like an eagle's sight beneath the world-illusion and saw it for what it is—a cosmic process of continual change which never comes to an end, a universal movement whose first impetus and final exhaustion will never be known, a flux of absolute duration and therefore unimaginable. And for the sage who attains to the knowledge of THAT which forever seems to be changing but forever paradoxically retains its own pure reality, for him as for the ignorant, the flux must go on. But it will go on here on this earth, not in the same mythical heaven or mirage-like hell. He will repeatedly have to take flesh, as all others will have to, so long as duration lasts, that is, forever. For he cannot sit apart like the yogi while his compassion is too profound to waste itself in mere sentiment. It demands the profound expression of sacrificial service in motion. His attitude is that so clearly described by a nineteenth-century agnostic whom religionists once held in horror, Thomas Huxley: 'We live in a world which is full of misery and ignorance, and the plain duty of each and all of us is to try to make the little corner he can influence somewhat less miserable and somewhat less ignorant than it was before he entered it.' The escape into Nirvana for him is the only escape into the inner realization of the truth whilst alive: it is not to escape from the external cycle of rebirths and deaths. It is a change of attitude. But that bait had to be held out to him at an earlier stage until his will and nerve were strong enough to endure this revelation. There is no escape except inwards. For the sage is too compassionate to withdraw into proud indifferentism and too understanding to rest completely satisfied with his own wonderful attainment. The sounds of sufferings of men, the ignorance that is the root of these sufferings, beat ceaselessly on the tympana of his ears. What can he do but answer, *and answer with his very life*—which he gives in perpetual reincarnation upon the cross of flesh as a vicarious sacrifice for others. It is thus alone that he achieves immortality, not by fleeing forever—as he could if he willed—into the Great Unconsciousness, but by suffering forever the pains and pangs of perpetual rebirth that he may help or guide his own.

XII.18.103

Whatever and whoever an adept brings into the Overself's light will eventually be conquered by that light.

XVI.25.150

The sage will not be primarily concerned with his own personal welfare, but then he will also not be primarily concerned with mankind's welfare. Both these duties find a place in his outlook, but they do not find a primary place. This is always filled by a single motive: to do the will, to express the inspiration of that greater self of which he is sublimely aware and to which he has utterly surrendered himself. This is a point whereon many students get confused or go astray. The sage does not stress altruism as the supreme value of life, nor does he reject egoism as the lowest value of life. He will act as the Overself bids him in each case, egotistically if it so wishes or altruistically if it so declares, but he will always act for its sake as the principal aim and by its light as the principal means.

XVI.25.155–6

The sage has conquered separativeness in his mind and realized the ALL as himself. The logical consequence is tremendous. It follows that there is no liberation from the round of births and rebirths for the sage; he has to go through it like the others. Of course, he does this with full understanding whereas they are plunged in darkness. But if he identifies himself with the All, then he can't desert but must go on to the end, working for the liberation of others in turn. This is his crucifixion, that being able to save others he is unable to save himself. 'And the scripture was fulfilled, which saith, "And he was numbered with the transgressors."' Why? Because compassion rules him, not the ego. Nobody is likely to want such a goal (until, indeed he is almost ready for it) so it is usually kept secret or symbolized. Again: 'For this is my blood of the new testament, which is shed for many for the remission of sins.'

XVI.25.146

There is no such act as a one-sided self-giving. Karma brings us back our due. He who spends his life in the dedicated service of philosophic enlightenment may reject the merely material rewards that this service could bring him, but he cannot reject the beneficent thoughts, the loving remembrances, the sincere veneration which those who have benefited sometimes send him. Such invisible rewards help him to atone more peacefully and less painfully for the strategic errors he has made, the tactical shortcomings he has manifested. Life is an arduous struggle for most people, but much more so for such a one who is always a hated target for the unseen powers of darkness. Do not hesitate to send him your silent humble blessing, therefore, and remember that Nature will not waste it. The enemies you are now struggling against within yourself he has already conquered, but the enemies he is now struggling against are beyond your present experience. He has won the right to sit by a hearth of peace. If he has made the greatest renunciation and does not do so, it is for your sake and for the sake of those others like you.

XV.24.65

From this lofty standpoint, the tenet of rebirth sinks to secondary place in the scale of importance. What does it matter whether one descends or not into the flesh if one always keeps resolute hold of the timeless Now? It can matter only to the little 'I', to the ignorant victim of ephemeral hopes and ephemeral fears, not to the larger 'I Am' which smiles down upon it.

XVI.28.32-3

The chasm between the Real and man seems entirely impassable. The intellect is conditioned by its own finitude, by its particular set of space and time perceptions. It is unable to function where absolutes alone reign. The infinite eternal and absolute existence eludes the grasp of man's logical thought. He may form mental pictures of it but at best they will be as far off from it as a photograph is far off from flesh and blood. Idea-worship is idol-worship. Everything else is an object of knowledge, experienced in a certain way by ourself as the knower of it; but the Infinite Real cannot be an object of anyone's knowledge simply because it cannot be conditioned in any way whatsoever. It is absolute. If it is to be known to all it must therefore be in a totally different way from that of ordinary experience. It is as inaccessible to psychic experience as it is impenetrable by thought and feeling. But although we may not directly know Reality, we may know that it is, and that in some mysterious way the whole cosmic existence roots from it. Thus whichever way man turns he, the finite creature, finds the door closed upon his face. The Infinite and Absolute Essence is forever beyond his vision, unreachable by his knowing capacity and inaccessible to his experience, and will forever remain so. The point is so subtle that, unless its development is expressed with great care here, it is likely to be misunderstood. Although man must pause here and say, with Socrates, 'None knoweth save God only'—for with this conception he has gone as far as human thought can grasp such mysteries—nevertheless he may know that the seers have not invented an imaginary Reality. He has neither been left alone in his mortality nor abandoned utterly to his finitude. The mysterious Godhead has provided a witness to its sacred existence, a Deputy to evidence its secret rulership. And that Witness and Deputy *can* be found for it sits imperishable in the very heart of man himself. It is indeed his true self, his immortal soul, his Overself. Although the ultimate principle is said to be inconceivable and unknowable, this is so only in relation to man's ordinary intellect and physical senses. It is not so in relation to a faculty in him which is still potential and unevolved—insight. If it be true that even no adept has ever seen the mysterious absolute, it is also true that he has seen the way it manifests its presence through something intimately emanated from it. If the nameless formless Void from which all things spring up and into which they go back is a world so subtle that it is not really intellectually understandable and so mysterious that it is not even mystically experienceable, we may however experience the strange atmosphere emanating from it, the unearthly aura signifying its hidden presence.

XVI.25.180–81

Much occult phenomena of the adept is performed without his conscious participation and 'above' his personal knowledge, as when various people claim to be aware of receiving help from him which he has no recollection of having

given. It is the Overself which is really giving the help, their
contact with him being merely like the switch which turns
on a light. But a switch is not the same as the electric current which, in this simile, represents the Overself. Yet a
switch is not less necessary in its own place. If he does not
use it, a man may grope in vain around a dark room and
not find what he is seeking there. The contact with an adept
turns some of the power that the adept is himself in touch
with into the disciple's direction. The flick of a switch is done
in a moment, whereas the current of light may flow into
the light bulb for many hours. The contact with an adept
takes a moment, but the spiritual current may emanate from
him for many years, even for a lifetime. Just as in the ordinary man's deep sleep no ego is working, so this is the perfect and highest state because no ego is working here either.
It reproduces deep sleep by eliminating egotism but transcends deep sleep by retaining consciousness. Thus it brings
the benefit without the spiritual blankess of deep sleep into
the waking state. If it be said, in criticism of his unawareness of so much occult phenomena manifesting in his name,
that this lessens his mental stature, he must answer that it
also preserves his mental sanity. How, with a thousand devotees, could he be attending to all of them at one and the same
time? By what magic could this be done and his peace
remain, his sanity be kept? God alone knows all things in
a mysterious everywhereness and everywhenness. How
could he be as God and yet remain as man, much more deal
with other men? For all occult phenomena belong to the
world of finite form, time and space, not to world of infinite
spirit, to illusion and not to reality. And, if, in further criticism, it be said that his unawareness makes him seem weaker
than an adept should be, he can only answer humbly that
because he has surrendered his personal rights he is weaker
and more helpless than the most ordinary man, that his situation was tersely described in Jesus' confession, 'I have no
power in myself, but only from the Father.'

XIII.21.108

The illuminate sees objects as other persons do, only his sense of materiality is destroyed, for he sees them too as *ideas*, unreal. The illuminate's viewpoint is *not* the yogi's viewpoint. The illuminate finds all the world in himself, says the *Gita*. This means he feels sympathetically at one with all creatures, even mosquitoes or snakes.

VIII.12.239

I wander farther afield and, overcome by a feeling of fatigue, throw myself upon the ground and listen to the hum of insects. The minutes pass and then I slowly become aware of a second sound. It is a kind of gentle swishing, yet so faint that it could be easily overlooked. Certainly if my corpse-like position did not bring my ears close to the ground, I could never hear the noise. I sit up suddenly and gaze around in a circular fashion. Through the bushes comes a gliding snake. The glittering, baleful eyes stare coldly and petrify me for a few moments. Why has Nature cursed this country with sneaking, crawling things? And then I remember the Buddha's injunction to be compassionate, to live and let live. Was he himself not shielded from the hot mid-day sun by a cobra which formed its hood into a canopy over the sage's head? Has not Nature provided a home for this snake equally as for me? Why need we look at each other with such trepidation? It rises from the ground in magnificent malignity to the height of my own head, a venomous and vertical creature whose neck gradually spreads out into a narrow hood marked with coloured spots. Instantly I direct my thought toward that Overself which pervades the creature confronting me no less than this body of mine. I perceive that this Self is one and the same and that the two forms appear *within* it. I sense that it is binding me to the other form in universal sympathy. My separateness, my fearfulness, even my repugnance and hatred, melt away. In that sublime unity, there is no second thing to arouse enmity . . . The snake passes on its way, and I am left safely alone. How much higher is this than the snake-magic which I learned in Egypt, how much more worthwhile! For the dervish who taught me his arcana of conquering cobras by occult powers now lies in a sandy grave outside Luxor, his face distorted by the agony of snake-bite, his twenty-year immunity lost in a single moment.

VIII.12.120

I walked among the sandy groves of the Philosophers. And I asked them, 'What is truth?'

And some said: 'It is thus.'

But others declared: 'It is not thus.'

And yet again: 'It is incomprehensible to man while he is yet mortal.'

I pondered upon these answers, yet I was not satisfied. Therefore it was that I fared farther. And I came to one who sat upon the stump of a tree trunk. And I saw that he was an old man who had been cast out of the ranks of the Philosophers because he could evolve no system.

Again I asked again: 'What is truth?'

He made no reply, but instead fixed his gaze on me. We sat silently together. His eyes gleamed with a strange lustre. And in that hour I came to know the meaning of truth. For his answer came through SILENCE.

XV.24.101

Many persons in different parts of the world and in different centuries have had glimpses of that other order of being which is their highest source, but how few are those who have succeeded in establishing themselves in continuous communion with that higher order, how rare is the feat? And who, having established himself therein, can find enough words to express what he now perceives and experiences? Words fall back; this is a plane not for them: this is a vast universal silence impregnated with consciousness which swallows every individualized being, for individuality cannot exist there. The established man can turn to it in this great silence and must himself remain silent to do it the honour it deserves. All language is so limited that it must seem blasphemy when put by side with this awed reverent stillness which is the proper form of worship here.

XV.24.100

The strange result of going deeper and deeper into the Real is that silence falls more and more as a curtain over his private experience and private thought. The strong urgency of communication which the missionary and the reformer feel, the strong need of expression which the artist and the writer have, trouble him no longer. The inner voice is tight-lipped, or speaks to him alone. He begins to see how much apostolic utterance is merely the overflow of personal emotion, how much artistic achievement is motivated by personal ambition, how much spiritual service is simply another phase of the ego adoring and serving itself. Thomas Aquinas came to such an insight late in life and he, the author of so many books dedicated to the glory of God, could never again write another line. Those who stand on the outside may consider such a severe restraint put upon oneself to be harsh and fanatical, perhaps even antisocial. But it is safe to say that all these critics have never tracked the ego to its secret lair, never had all movement of their individual will stopped by the divine Stillness.

XV.24.85

Far from the arguments of mind-narrowed men, he will find himself without a supporting group in the end. He is to meet God alone, for *all* his attention is to be held—so fully that there is nothing and no one else. Thus the three become two, who in turn become the One, which it always is. Truth is no longer needed; its seeker has vanished. The great Silent Timelessness reigns.

XV.24.96

It is a sweet peace gracious beyond all telling.

XV.24.101

We have heard much about the sayings of Jesus, nothing about his silences. Yet it was from the latter that they came and in the latter that he himself *lived*.

XV.24.96

'I, the Homeless, have My home in each person's heart.' This is what the Great Silence told me.

XV.24.93

The stillness is not experienced in the same way as a mere lazy and idle reverie: it is dynamic, creative, and healing. The presence of one man who is able to attain it is a gift, a blessing, to all other men, though they know it not.

BIBLIOGRAPHY

1. Books published during Paul Brunton's lifetime

A Search in Secret India (London: Rider & Co., 1934).

The Secret Path (London: Rider & Co., 1935).

A Search in Secret Egypt (London: Rider & Co., 1936).

A Message from Arunachala (London: Rider & Co., 1936).

A Hermit in the Himalayas (Madras, 1936; London: Rider & Co., 1949).

The Quest of the Overself (London: Rider & Co., 1937).

The Inner Reality (London: Rider & Co., 1939). Published in the USA by E.P. Dutton as *Discover Yourself*.

Indian Philosophy and Modern Culture (London: Rider & Co., 1939).

The Hidden Teaching Beyond Yoga (London: Rider & Co., 1941).

The Wisdom of the Overself (London: Rider & Co., 1943).

The Spiritual Crisis of Man (London: Rider & Co., 1952).

2. Books published posthumously

Essays on the Quest (London: Rider & Co., 1984).

The Notebooks of Paul Brunton (Burdett, NY: Larson Publications, 1984-9).

Vol. 1 *Perspectives*

A representative survey of all twenty-eight categories in the 'Ideas' series.

Vol. 2 *The Quest*

Containing Category 1

Vol. 3 *Practices for the Quest/Relax and Retreat*

Containing Categories 2 and 3

Vol. 4 *Meditation/The Body*
Containing Categories 4 and 5
  Vol. 5 *Emotions and Ethics/The Intellect*
Containing Categories 6 and 7
  Vol. 6 *The Ego/From Birth to Rebirth*
Containing Categories 8 and 9
  Vol. 7 *Healing of the Self/The Negatives*
Containing Categories 10 and 11
  Vol. 8 *Reflections on My Life and Writings*
Containing Category 12
  Vol. 9 *Human Experience/The Arts in Culture*
Containing Categories 13 and 14
  Vol. 10 *The Orient*
Containing Category 15
  Vol. 11 *The Sensitives*
Containing Category 16
  Vol. 12 *The Religious Urge/The Reverential Life*
Containing Categories 17 and 18
  Vol. 13 *Relativity, Philosophy, and Mind*
Containing Categories 19, 20, and 21: The Reign of Relativity; What is Philosophy? Mentalism
  Vol. 14 *Inspiration and the Overself*
Containing Category 22
  Vol. 15 *Advanced Contemplation/The Peace Within You*
Containing Categories 23 and 24
  Vol. 16 *Enlightened Mind, Divine Mind*
Containing Categories 25, 26, 27, and 28: World Mind in Individual Mind; World-Idea; World-Mind; The Alone.

3. About Paul Brunton

Paul Brunton: A Personal View by Kenneth Thurston Hurst (Burdett, NY: Larson Publications, 1989; distributed in the UK by Element Books).

INDEX

Of further interest...

JACOB BOEHME
ESSENTIAL READINGS
Edited and introduced
by Robin Waterfield

As a cobbler in Görlitz, Jacob Boehme (1575-1624) came into contact with many great thinkers who sought refuge from the Roman Church and Reformation groups in post-Luther Germany. Gradually his experiences led him to become one of the most influential mystics of the Reformation era.

Boehme was persecuted by the new establishment — not for his ideas but for what was seen as his presumption of writing from his lowly social position. His intention, however, was not to preach but to stimulate the light of truth in the individual through his 'esoteric psychology', and his goal was to inspire his readers to form a personal relationship with Christ. That he succeeded in his endeavours becomes clear when one reads these, his ESSENTIAL READINGS.

PARACELSUS
ESSENTIAL READINGS
Selected and translated
by Nicholas Goodrick-Clarke

Paracelsus (1493-1541) was a stormy light in the Reformation world. He became a controversial figure by rejecting the slavish dependence of contemporary medicine on abstract reason and classical texts: he wanted to found a new medical science based on experiment, observation, chemical remedies and Renaissance philosophy. Rooted in the spiritual relation between man and the cosmos, his ideas have remained influential long after his death, and he is known today as 'the father of modern medicine'.

With the growing interest in the esoteric and in alternative medicine (especially homoeopathy), Paracelsus' magical and holistic approach is once again highly topical. Tracing his boyhood interest in natural science, his education and journeys throughout Europe, his mission as a lay-preacher and healer, and his conflict with the authorities, this anthology brings his work to the general reader for the first time, showing his importance in the history of ideas and his relevance today.

RUDOLF STEINER ESSENTIAL READINGS
Selected and edited by Richard Seddon

Rudolf Steiner (1861-1925) was a supersensitive with a scientific education, a pairing which enabled him to combine both poles of life in a unique way. His descriptions of spiritual research were as systematic as any science, and his rigorous path of self-development clearly mapped out for anyone to follow.

Anthroposophy, the path of wisdom and knowledge he initiated, is man-centred and holistic, and this volume plots its philosophy — man's struggle to attain full spiritual stature through the practical application of the forces brought by Christ. Steiner saw the spirit as the creative element in evolution, and his work is now being accepted as a practical vitalizing force for today's world.